Print with Collage & Stitch

Print with Collage & Stitch

Techniques for Mixed-Media Printmaking

Val Holmes

INTERWEAVE
interweave.com

First published in the United States in 2012 by

Interweave Press LLC
201 East Fourth Street
Loveland, CO 80537
www.interweave.com

ISBN: 978-1-59668-589-5

Reproduction by Rival Colour Ltd, UK
Printed by 1010 Printing International Ltd, China

10 9 8 7 6 5 4 3 2 1

Library of Congress Cataloging-in-Publication Data

Holmes, Val.
  Print with collage and stitch : techniques for mixed-media printmaking / Val Holmes.
     pages cm
  Includes bibliographical references and index.
  ISBN 978-1-59668-589-5 (pbk.)
  1. Collagraph printing--Technique. I. Title.
  NE2232.H65 2012
  760--dc23
                                    2011052798

CONTENTS

INTRODUCTION

What is collagraphy?

Traditional printing methods

Most print techniques require the printmaker to remove areas from the surface of the chosen material, so that the printing surface is incised rather than raised, in order to create the printing plate. The plate may then be printed intaglio: this means that the holes or lines created in the plate will be filled with ink. This is done by applying ink and then wiping off the excess from the main surface of the plate, leaving ink only in the incisions. During the printing process the press applies the necessary weight and pressure so that the paper finds the ink and reproduces the image drawn into the plate.

Intaglio printing is usually associated with etched metal, a process that is achieved either by taking away the surface with special tools or by a method known as

aqua forte. In this technique the metal is first coated with varnish into which the design is drawn, and then the plate is placed in a bath of acid or a similar substance in order to etch into the areas where the varnish has been removed. For intaglio printing a press is essential.

The plate can also be made to be printed in relief. In this case the ink will be applied, usually with a roller, to those parts of the plate left in relief, rather than into those taken away. The paper is then placed onto the inked plate, to be printed with some pressure.

Relief printing is most often associated with woodblock or lino printing, in which areas of the material are gouged out, leaving a structure in relief for printing. For relief printing, a press is not essential.

Marshes in the Mist by Claude Vallin. Etching from a copper plate, done with the *aqua forte* technique. The ink was in the crevices of the plate and an etching press with great pressure was used to force the paper into them to find the ink.

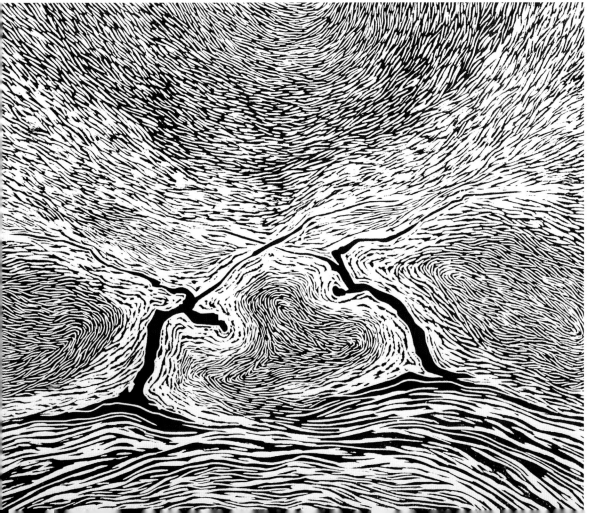

Dancing Vines by Claire Fauchard. Lino print. A great deal of lino was removed, leaving fine black areas.

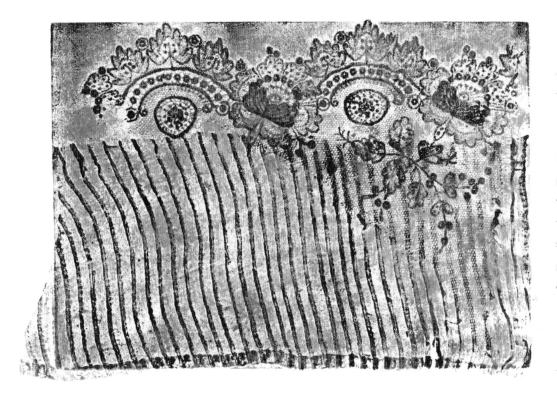

From Riches to Rags.
The plate was made on card, using lace and pin-tucked fabric, which was protected with gesso before printing. The gold for the intaglio printing was pushed into the crevices with a brush; the pink was then rolled onto the relief surface. The plate was printed in one step under an etching press.

Collagraphy

Collagraphy is different from the above methods because it generally involves adding elements to the plate instead of taking them away. Different materials can be used to form the base structure of the plate, from cardboard to wood, plastic, to old lino. As for what can be added, the range is almost as large and varied as the number of artists working in this medium. Classically, cut card and carborundum powders are most commonly used, but acrylic texture mediums, sandpaper, string, threads, fabric, rice, and various organic materials can also be used, all of which will be discussed in this book. The resulting plate can be printed using either an intaglio method or in relief, or both at the same time, and it may be printed with or without a press. The resulting print is called a collagraph. Different tonal effects are achieved according to the depth and type of relief, and with the highly textured surfaces that are possible.

What makes this way of printing interesting for the artist or textile artist is that a number of pieces can be created with the same image from one plate, just as with other methods of printing. These pieces may be identical, in which case they can be numbered and sold as such. This is the advantage that all artists working with printing techniques have: the ability to produce serial pieces of work that are therefore less expensive for the buyer.

But there is another advantage that I consider more important for the artist on a personal voyage of discovery. Instead of printing the plate with the same colors on the same kind of paper, experiments can be undertaken with different color schemes, different papers and even different fabrics. Seeing the same image treated with different colours can be very inspirational for future work, either for print ideas or as an influence in your more classic art or embroidery production. For the textile artist there is also the advantage that different renditions of the same image, created by using varying colours, papers or fabrics, can all be treated differently. For example, certain prints could be left as simple untouched images, whereas others could be lightly or heavily embroidered, or appliqué or other embellishments could be included. In this way you will learn more about a particular image and how to respond to it.

Rocks. The plate was made on card with acrylic gel medium. It was printed on a press using oil–based ink. Machine–stitched dyed cotton scrim and inked tarlatan were added to the print.

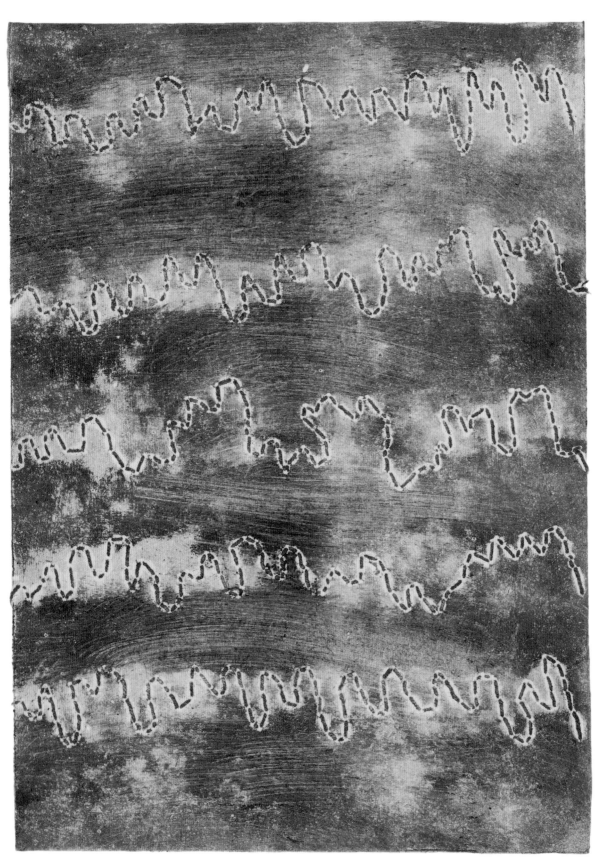

Vague écriture.
The title is a play
on words, the
French *vague*
meaning both
indistinct and
wave, and
écriture meaning
writing – hence
wave writing or
vague writing.
The marks were
influenced by a
drawing done on
a beach where
wavelets
brushed some
rocks. The
stitching directly
onto card, using
free–motion
embroidery, was
worked with a
thick sewing
thread. The card
and stitching
were protected
with gesso
before printing.

A little bit of history

Elementary contemporary collagraphy techniques can be seen in prints from as early as the late 19th century, when Pierre Roche (1855–1922), a student of the French artist Auguste Rodin (1840-1917), started experimenting with plaster as a print relief medium, and later on with an adhesive. But a more widespread use of collagraphic methods for print production dates from around the 1920s, when many innovative artists of the day, such as Pablo Picasso (1881–1973), began using collage as an artistic medium. It didn't take long before printmakers and painters interested in print started to collage cloth, metal, or sand to texture their plates. The production of cheap strong adhesives was influential in the development of the medium for some, but for the German Expressionist artist Rolf Nesch (1893–1975) these were unnecessary, as he drilled holes in his plates, threaded metal wire through them, or soldered on metal shapes and wires. His plates were so heavily in relief that he needed a large number of protective felts between the plate and the roller of the press in order to protect the roller. He called his pieces 'Metal Prints' and there are examples of his work in the British Museum in London.

The term 'collagraphy' is attributed to the printmaker and educator Glen Alps (1914–96), who developed the technique with his students while teaching at the School of Art at the University of Washington in Seattle, USA. He found the technique particularly useful because it allowed an artist to work spontaneously in print and to realize visual ideas rapidly. He soon became aware that a name was required for the process, and he coined the word 'collagraphy', from the Greek *koll* or *kollo*, meaning glue, and *graph*, meaning the activity of drawing. He is also attributed with the acceptance and dissemination of the process as an art form, as he created an enormous number of prints, which were exhibited in national exhibitions, and in 1966 made a 20-minute film entitled *The Collagraph*, in which he demonstrated the technique. He was apparently an inspirational teacher, and many of his students continued to develop the techniques further.

The rise of collagraphy continued with the advent of Pop Art and the increasing popularity of the print process. Today many artists employ the technique, if only in the use of carborundum as an addition to etched plates, although many others are developing the medium further with the improvement of glues and acrylic pastes.

There are probably as many ways to approach this fantastically diverse artistic medium as there are practitioners, so I will admit straightaway that this book is a very personal one. I will be looking at the materials and methods that are generally used in collagraphy, and the different printing techniques, but above all I intend to share my own approach, which is that of a textile artist and embroiderer, and as such, of course, a little out of the ordinary. As many of my plates include stitching but no glue, I decided to coin the term "brodagraphy," having researched the possible origins of the word "embroidery".

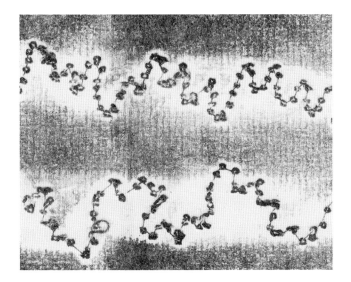

Vague écriture. This is a detail of a reverse–side print of the piece – the burrs made by the machine needle on the reverse side can be seen. The bobbin thread was much finer, so it becomes a very delicate line.

CHAPTER ‹ 1 ›
MAKING THE PLATE

Materials suitable for making the plate

The first step in the printmaking process is to make the object that will be inked or painted before being applied to the textile or paper surface to leave behind an imprint of the marks that have been made on it. This is called the *plate*. Bear in mind that all marks made on the plate will be reversed, as in a mirror, when printed.

Artists use many different materials to make plates, and each has advantages and disadvantages, particularly in respect of the longevity of the plate and its ease of use. Each artist will have a preference for one material over another according to the demands and criteria for his or her own production requirements.

The longevity of the plate – that is, the number of prints that can be successfully printed from it – will

depend on the materials used to make it and the way in which it is protected with varnishes or similar products. Some collagraphy artists manage to obtain up to 100 prints off the same plate, while others may print as few as five. The choices made will also affect whether or how well the plate can be cleaned between each printing session. If printing only five or ten prints from a plate, it will be more economical in both time and materials to do this in one session, so as not to have to worry about cleaning the plate when the print run is finished. If a large series of identical prints is required, it may be preferable to be able to clean the plate and reuse it later.

For your first plates and experiments the notion of longevity may be a little academic. Trying out different

Urban Landscape.
The plate is a drink can embroidered with a set machine stitch (see page 17) and pieces of masking tape were added. It was printed with an etching press on watercolor paper, using water-washable ink.

surfaces on the plate and exploring the results that these produce in relation to your own imagery or ideas will be more rapid if you restrict the number of prints to a modest quantity – say, between five and fifteen. This will be enough to enable you to experiment with different papers, fabrics, and colors, and to follow up the print process with stitch and other embellishments if desired.

The following sections look at the materials that are generally used for collagraphy. Initially, keep your choices simple, so that you can enjoy your experiments.

Cardboard

A rigid cardboard can prove a very useful base for a plate, and it is cheap and readily available. I use matboard as this is easy to sew through. The disadvantage with cardboard is that even the most rigid type is a little soft, and a printing press will gradually squash the elements that have been added to it into the surface of the cardboard, resulting in the loss of the design's details over only a fairly small number of prints. To date, the maximum I have achieved with this method has been around twenty prints.

The cardboard can be protected with varnish or gesso and carefully cleaned for reuse at a later date. It is possible to protect cardboard enough to be able to remove water-based ink; oil-based ink can be messier and more difficult to use, as more time and effort are required to remove it (see page 39). Therefore, when using oil-based ink, it is best to do the complete print run in one go. If working with both water-based and oil-based media, use the water-based medium first, clean and dry the plate, and then use the oil-based medium.

A cardboard plate has the advantage of being flexible, and because of this it can be used with various types of home-based presses, such as mangles or even some pasta-making machines. Cardboard plates may need special preparation before being printed, however (see page 32).

Four Trees. This shows a used cardboard plate – the image is now too flat for printing. The trees were made on Thermogauze vanishing muslin, which disintegrates when heated with a heat gun or iron. Some of the muslin fibers were left attached to the trees to create more texture or twigs on the branches. These trees were glued to cardboard, which was then protected with gesso. The plate was printed with oil-based ink under an etching press; it was not cleaned after use as it could not be reused.

Cork tiles

Cork tiles provide a hard but flexible surface for a plate, and as they are not very thick they will adapt well to all methods of printing. The most satisfactory type of cork tile is the one that is sold for use in model-making, as it is fine and very flexible. The texture of the cork itself can be exploited if desired, or it can be covered with other textural materials. It is easy to cut into or make holes in cork, and embroidery by hand or machine is also relatively easy. The materials added to cork squash less easily into its firm surface, so a plate made with a cork tile can have a longer life than a cardboard one.

Orchard in Autumn.
A print from a cork mat with stitching and applied silk. Water-washable ink was used.

Plastic

From my initial experiments with handstitching on fine Perspex (see page 68), I have found plastic interesting for the way that ink behaves on it: if you apply gesso to the plastic surface, it retains ink; if you don't, the ink can easily be wiped off. Other types of plastic that can be used include thick plastic bags or the kind of plastic used to protect tables under tablecloths. The plastic bags that my watercolor or printing paper is delivered in are very useful. These can be stitched into relatively easily, but be aware that the flexibility of plastic can compromise any materials glued onto it.

A plastic plate is also easy to wipe and clean. This quality can make it interesting for line work, as ink will attach itself to any stitching and the plastic can then be wiped clean of any remaining ink, leaving ink only on the stitching. The stitching will not stick to paper, so does not need to be protected in any way.

Vines. A print from machine stitching on plastic, printed with a flower press on 40gsm Japanese paper with water–washable ink.

Wood–type products

Different types of fiberboard, plywood, and chipboard can all be used as a base for a plate. Medium-density fiberboard (MDF) is often used as a substitute for wood in woodblock printing as it offers a perfectly flat surface that is easy to cut into with gouging tools. Other wood-based products, such as plywood, often have an interesting textured surface that in itself will offer an aesthetic quality to the print. Holes can be drilled for sewn attachments or added texture, and other materials can be added relatively easily with glue – wood glue or PVA glue adhere well to wood surfaces. The surface will need to be varnished with a resistant varnish if the plate is to be kept and reused. The resulting plate will last well, although its longevity will also depend on the elements that have been added to it.

The thickness and lack of flexibility of wood products may cause a problem with some types of press, and it will be impossible to use them with a home-based press such as a mangle or a pasta-making machine. Even with professional presses problems can be experienced with the thickness of the plate, so check the maximum that is possible with your press carefully. If you are using methods of printing that don't require a press, wood-based plates will prove quite useful because of their rigidity.

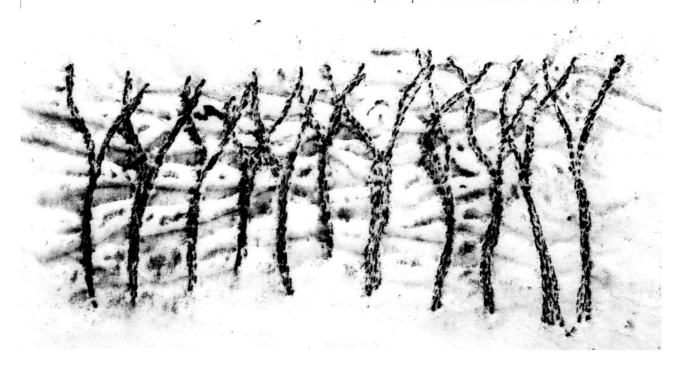

Metal

Metal has the advantage of being a robust medium that can be cleaned again and again. Gluing elements to its surface can be a little more problematic, however, as certain glues will not withstand the same degree of cleaning that the metal plate will. For this reason it may be preferable to use water-based ink or water-washable etching ink (see pages 42–44).

Metal plates are frequently used by collagraphy artists who mix their collagraph practice with normal etching techniques such as *aqua forte* or direct engraving. Gluing carborundum to the plate is an initial step towards collagraphy for many such artists, who may subsequently be inspired to add more materials to the plate.

The metal plate can be protected with varnish if necessary, although this will depend on the materials that have been added to it, and it will last for a large number of prints. Zinc and copper are traditionally used by etching artists for making plates, but I have one friend who works almost exclusively with steel and another who uses old tin cans, opened and flattened, for direct engraving.

Obviously, these thick metal surfaces are impossible to stitch into by machine, and they can accept hand stitching only if drilled with the appropriate holes first. Drink cans, however, are soft and flexible enough to be sewn into by machine, and it is fairly easy to punch holes into them for hand stitching. Squashed cans may create interesting patterns for printing, whereas cans that have been carefully preserved may provide flat surfaces that can be wiped clean easily. I have found that beer cans are easier to stitch into by machine than soft drink cans, because the metal is finer.

Other materials

There are very few limits to what can be tried as a base for a printing plate. I have used watercolor paper, Lutradur, stitched fabric (protected with gesso) and some organic materials. With certain surfaces longevity becomes an issue, to the point where the work involved in preparing a plate for just one or two prints may not really

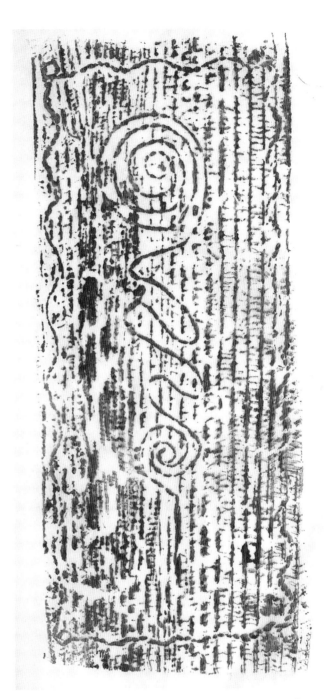

The Sun's Tale. This was worked in cable stitch on an exotic leaf taken from a florist's display. It was printed on 40gsm Japanese paper with acrylic ink, using a baren and spoon to avoid flattening and breaking the textures of the leaf.

seem worth the effort. Some experiments may even not withstand a print in a press, although they may be all right for a hand-printing method. If a material looks interesting as a starting point for a plate, it is worth giving it a go on a small scale first, just to see what the result may be.

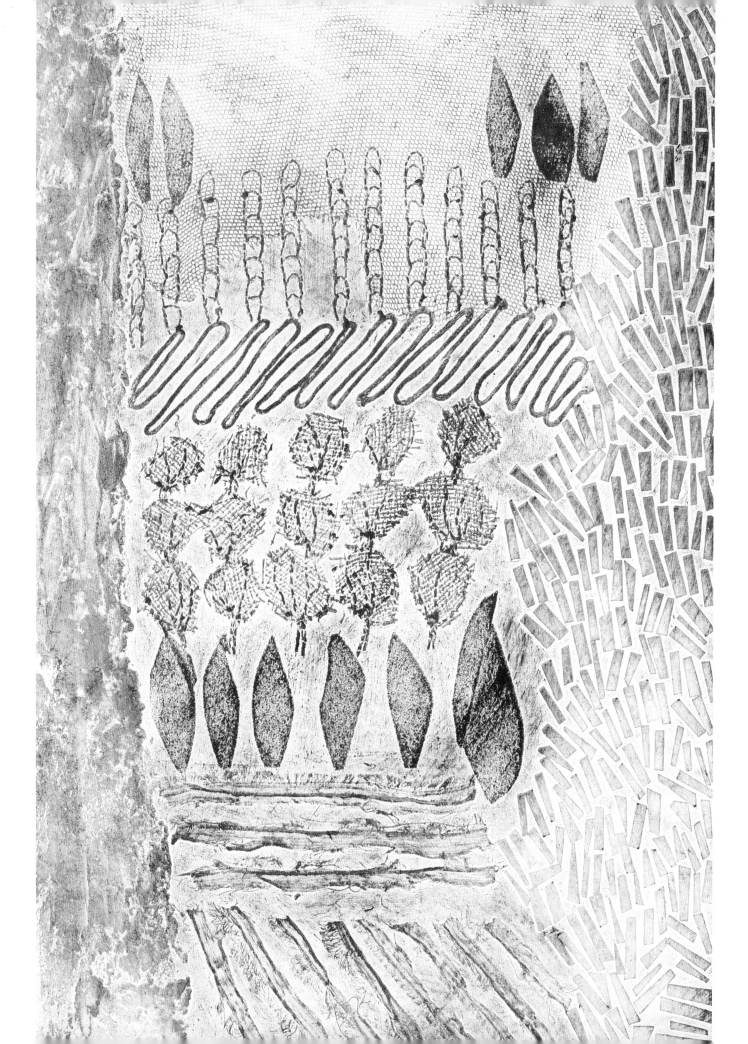

Adding to the plate

The range of materials suitable for adding to a plate is almost as wide as your imagination. Again, though, there is the problem of longevity. Some materials will make more prints than others, so try out ones that offer interesting textures and see what they withstand. Some materials that work well when printing with a press will not give a good result if you are using hand-printing methods without a press, and vice versa. Some organic materials, for example, are just too delicate to be passed through a press.

Carborundum

Carborundum is a compound of silicon and carbon that is produced artificially. Its first use, at the end of the 19th century, was as an abrasive material, and it is now widely used in many industries. It can be bought in powder form, in fine, medium, or coarse grain, from etching suppliers, but it is also worth experimenting with emery paper and sandpaper, in which carborundum or similar materials are already glued onto a paper base.

The powder can be sprinkled onto wet glue, such as PVA, or strong double-sided tape. It can also be mixed with acrylic mediums, paints, and pastes for texture and then painted onto the plate or applied with a palette knife. The advantage of this medium over sand, for example, is that the grain size purchased is consistent and the resulting texture will therefore be even. This will be easier for printing plates that are to be burnished by hand.

Emery paper and sandpaper can be cut to the shape required and glued onto a plate. Any such paper that has already been used for DIY purposes can be interesting to use on a plate, as the worn areas will provide different textures. Finer emery and sandpapers can actually be stitched onto the plate, but make sure that you clean the sewing machine well afterwards.

San Gimignano. This image, shown here in full, was printed with a card plate, using oil-based ink on etching paper, printed on an etching press.

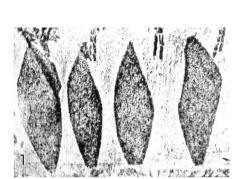

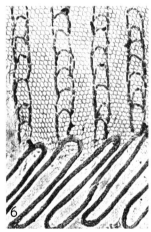

San Gimignano details

1. Double-sided tape cut to the right shape for the cypress trees was stuck to the card and sprinkled with carborundum powder.
2. This shows textured acrylic paste.
3. Cut pieces of thin cardboard applied with PVA glue.
4. Torn silk applied with PVA glue.
5. Open-weave linen fabric stitched into place.
6. Soft embroidery cotton and embroidery on net, applied with glue.

Acrylic paste and gel medium

There is a huge range of textured acrylic mediums, which are generally quite expensive but work well, particularly when printing with a press. You can experiment with home-made versions by using cheap acrylic paint or PVA glue and textured materials, such as sand, carborundum, grains, rice, oats, plaster, and so on. Whether bought or homemade, these materials can be scraped onto the plate with a palette knife, and even drawn into with a sharp or rounded tool while still wet. Try to limit the amount of relief if you are printing with a hand-burnishing method or roller.

Acrylic gel medium creates a surface that wipes quite nicely: color can be left on the gel medium where required and wiped off elsewhere, producing subtle results.

Borderline. The plate was made on cardboard with acrylic gel medium, open-weave fabrics, and silk waste. It was printed with an etching press, using water-washable ink on etching paper.

Seascape. The plaster was applied to the plate with a spatula to create texture. The image was printed with an etching press, using water-washable ink on etching paper.

Plaster

Some of the very first experiments with collagraphy were made by sculpting plaster. When using plaster – whether sculpted or textured while wet, or worked into or sanded when dry – the plate needs to be of a fairly rigid material to prevent cracking. Card will be adequate if you are applying wet plaster, but use something more rigid if the plaster is to be sculpted or sanded once dry.

The type of product used as a filler for holes in plasterwork is ideal for adding to a plate as it is easy to apply and sand down, and it is also slightly pliable. It has a longer drying time than ordinary plaster of Paris, so will allow greater flexibility when being used. The plaster can be applied with a spatula or similar implement, textured with any interesting tool, have objects pressed into it to leave imprints, and have materials such as sand, carborundum, or oat flakes added to it to give it more texture. With or without added textures, it makes an excellent ground for a print – as easy to use as acrylic pastes, but more economical. Generally, very little plaster is needed to cover a plate, so take this into consideration when mixing up the quantity required. The resulting plate will take the weight and pressure of an etching press, but can also be used if you are printing by hand, using a baren and spoon – and even, if the plaster is very textured, fingers.

Orchard in Winter. I was trying to achieve the same effect as a woodblock print. Thin card was glued to a card plate and carborundum was added in some areas. The plate could be printed either with a baren or the etching press.

Thin cardboard

Great results can be obtained by simply adding thin, very firm cardboard to a plate. By cutting out the shapes required and gluing them onto the plate to make a design, you can achieve a result that is a little like a linocut or woodblock print. The ink rolls easily onto the surface and the plate is easy to print off, particularly with handprinting methods. A press can also be used with this technique, but the card will crush more rapidly than with a roller or hand burnishing, so fewer prints will be obtained from the plate.

Textured paper and wallpaper

Textured paper and wallpaper can make interesting additions to a plate. The hardness of the chosen paper can be very deceptive, so it is always a little difficult to predict how many prints you will be able to achieve from a plate made in this way. When using a printing press it is possible to print intaglio and in relief at the same time with textured paper. This technique is covered in more detail in Chapter 5.

Corrugated cardboard

Corrugated cardboard is flattened pretty quickly by a printing press, but the results can be interesting. Using a roller or hand burnishing will preserve the quality of the cardboard for more prints. When using a printing press you might want to consider the virtue of the piece being printed in intaglio and relief at the same time. This process is covered in more detail in Chapter 5.

Glue

The solid glue from a glue gun can prove long-lasting. It can be left as a designed string straight from the glue gun, or marks can be made into the glue using tools such as forks or palette knives.

PVA glue

Any number of interesting textural materials can be glued onto or mixed into PVA glue or acrylic medium. Just try anything and everything you have on hand. PVA glue can also be used on its own to make textures and marks. It can be added in drips or with a brush, and you can also draw or comb into it. If it is used thickly, it will take some time to dry – leave it until it is completely clear before attempting to print with it.

Refugees. Drips of PVA glue on a cardboard plate. This was printed with an etching press, using water-washable ink on etching paper. It also printed well by hand.

The Sun's Tale. Cable stitch and stitching with a quilting thread in free-motion stitching on embossed paper. This particular print is the eighth in a series of twelve prints. The colors became more and more developed as the series went on. This was printed with an etching press on 300gsm etching paper, using oil-based ink.

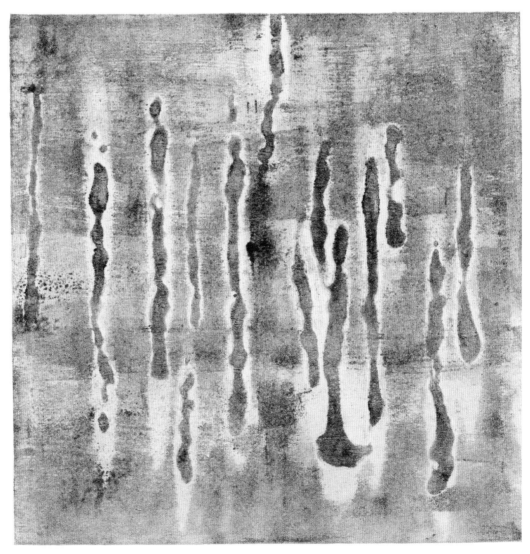

Threads and stitching

All types of threads can be glued into place or attached with double-sided tape. For clear results it is best to choose threads that are firm, not fluffy. If a thread is fluffy or uneven, then make sure that it is well protected with gesso or varnish. Stitching can be done by hand or machine. Care should be taken with the choice of thread to create a firm line: fine machine-embroidery threads will flatten quickly, so choose strong sewing threads or thicker quilting or topstitch threads. Cable stitch worked from the back with thick hand-embroidery threads on the bobbin also works well. This topic will be covered in more detail in Chapter 3.

String and threads

Smooth or rough string can create interesting line designs on a plate. Although string can be glued into place with PVA glue, it is much easier to use double-sided tape. Choose a carpet-quality double-sided tape so that it holds well. Threads can also be used, and I particularly like soft embroidery cotton as this has a good firm line quality as well as longevity for printing. Lines between strips of double-sided tape will show up if you are printing with a press, so take suitable precautions to camouflage them or make sure that they add something to the design.

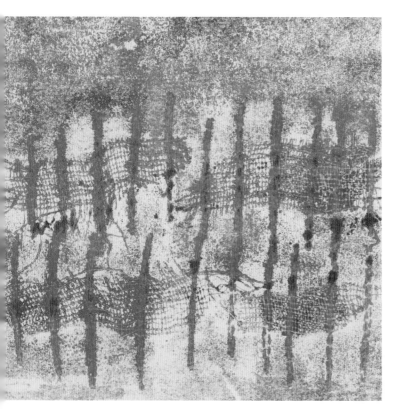

Oyster Park. Lines of stitching hold in place a fine-weave linen scrim. This was worked on carborundum paper and the design was printed on watercolor paper with oil-based ink on an etching press.

Wood. Soft embroidery cotton stuck to double-sided carpet tape on a card plate, protected with gesso. The plate was printed with oil-based ink on an etching press, in both relief and intaglio. The green color is on the relief parts of the plate – that is, on the cotton thread. The orange color is on the areas between the thread.

Lace

There are many different types of lace – from handmade bobbin lace, needle-made lace, tatting and crochet lace, to various types of industrial lace and sewing-machine-made lace. The important factors here are the clarity of the lace, the thickness of the threads, their quality and thread type, and the thickness of the lace itself. Linen threads make a very firm lace for printing with, whereas some handmade tatting or crochet laces can be heavy, clumsy and unclear in collagraphy. Other laces, machine or handmade, may have threads that are too soft to withstand many passes under a press, although they will accept hand-printing techniques if they are flat and even.

It is difficult to assess how many prints can be achieved from a given lace, or how clear the prints will be, unless the composition of the threads is known. It is a good idea to build up experience of the different qualities of lace and the results they will give by making a sample plate with many different types of lace. For future work it will then be possible to mix laces that are likely to have a similar longevity. You will also discover that some laces can be printed with hand-printing methods, whereas others need the pressure of the press to ensure that the details show up. An even depth will be essential for a plate that is to be hand-printed, but is unimportant if you are using an etching press. Broderie anglaise can give good results in hand-printing. Patience and a combination of techniques, using a baren, spoon and even fingers, will be required for good hand-printing.

Reflections of Venice. The starting point was a watercolor painting of water reflections in Venice. One of the laces used is Venetian needle–made lace. Other laces on the plate include industrial laces, bobbin lace, needle-made lace, and broderie anglaise. The laces were stitched to card and protected with gesso. The plate was printed with oil-based ink on an etching press.

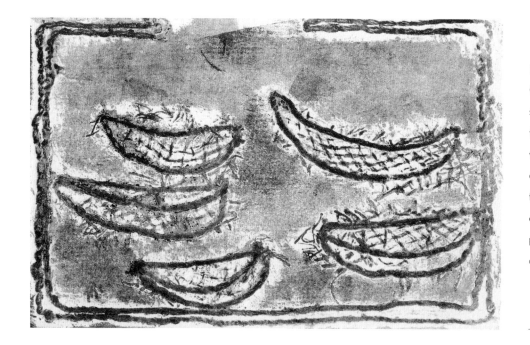

Port with Fishing Boats. Coarse linen scrim was stitched onto card from the front of the plate. The plate was then turned over and cable stitch was stitched from the back with soft embroidery cotton. It was printed with oil-based ink on an etching press.

Open-weave fabrics

As with lace, the quality and type of thread used to make the fabric will have a bearing on its clarity and longevity in printing. Linen gives excellent results and the imprint of the threads will last for many prints.

Olive Trees. Carborundum on double-sided tape on a silk crepe base stuck to card. Additional pieces of silk satin were added in strips. The plate was printed with oil-based ink on an etching press.

Silk

Silk retains color extremely well, so it can be used to create very black or strong-colored areas. The mezzotint etching process relies on an overworked plate to produce a print that is almost black. Silk is an ideal base to achieve this. You can then change the silk in some way, perhaps by creasing it or in the way that you protect it; or you can stitch on it to modulate the degree of blackness or intense color. Silk does not need protecting with a varnish as it will not stick to the paper, and for this reason it can be interesting to use untreated silk for the intense blacks and varnish only the other areas of the plate.

Other fabrics

Many fabrics, such as damask, have a texture that may well be worth trying on a plate. Synthetic fabrics, such as polyester organdy and Lutradur, can produce interesting surfaces without being heat-treated, but if they are distressed with a heat tool even more texture can be created. However, care needs to be taken in the use of this texture if the result is not to be one big mess!

Quarry Landscape. Burnt Lutradur with holes and blisters, glued to a card plate with a strip of satin glued across. The plate was protected with gesso and printed with oil-based ink on an etching press.

E/A   Val Flokes

Organic materials

Fantastic textures can be found in natural objects, but unfortunately very few of these actually print well in collagraphy. Several problems occur with wonderfully textured natural objects: first, it is not possible to ink up the object sufficiently to be able to get a good print – it may well be too textured or uneven; second, the object may be too thick to pass under the press or too deep to be included with other items; and third, the object may be too fragile to stay in one piece if passed through a printing press, in which case the prints obtained can become quite messy fairly quickly. Organic materials are less robust under a printing press, but their detailed textures may not print so well with hand-printing methods.

A good way forward when working with interesting organic textures and objects is to try printing in the first instance with a hand method, using a spoon or a baren, for instance. By doing this, the fragility of the object can be felt without having to worry too much about its thickness. After a trial run the object could be printed on a press and perhaps incorporated into a plate with other textures and surfaces.

I have found very few leaves that are capable of withstanding the press. In the case of skeleton leaves, for example, although varnishes can help, it is difficult not to lose details. Hand printing, however, works well.

Seed Head. The seed head was stitched and then glued into place with a generous quantity of PVA glue. A print was taken, using a baren, spoon, and fingers, with acrylic ink on fine 40gsm Japanese paper. The yellow and green inks were squeezed onto the glass ink plate and rolled onto a sponge roller, which was then applied to the plate. As the two colors had not been mixed together on the glass plate prior to printing, the colors are both distinct and mixed on the inked-up plate and on the print.

A print taken from a card of buttons, using water-washable ink on an etching press.

Buttons, beads and sequins

Such objects can be broken up by a press, so be aware of this. A further problem in the case of buttons is that if placed in isolation on a plate, they are very likely to pierce the felts as you roll the plate through the press, although I have managed to avoid this when the buttons were very close together. To create the effect of a button on a plate, use card and stitching as this will not damage the felts. These objects do not present the same difficulties with hand printing, but fine, tough paper must be used in order to print from them successfully, and care taken so as not to tear the paper.

The reverse side of the print, using water-washable ink on an etching press.

Metal parts

It is important to choose suitable metal parts so that the different depths in the plate do not cause problems, but if care is taken in this respect, hand printing can be successful. Printing with metal parts on a press can ruin the felts and even the roller. To avoid this eventuality, use lots of layers of felt (three to six, depending on the depth required) and old felts or blankets underneath the decent felts so as not to ruin these, which are expensive to replace.

Epoxy resins are very useful for sticking metal to surfaces, or use stitch if appropriate. The advantage of a plate with metal parts on it is that it will last for a large number of prints.

Sticky tapes

Different sticky tapes give different results, according to their ability to retain the ink. They range from ordinary sticky tape, which wipes clean very easily, to masking tape, which holds more ink, and sticking plasters, which behave differently depending on whether they are plastic- or fabric-based. Parcel wrapping tape can be wiped clean, but may pleat as you put it down. Double-sided tape can be used to hold down other objects.

Summary of materials

The table opposite will give you some idea of which materials can or cannot be added to a plate successfully (they will give good, reproducible results in the given circumstances). Even if I find a result unclear or messy, you may find it useful as a starting point for something else. Printing with a press will allow both relief and intaglio printing, whereas with hand-printing methods relief printing is more likely, although more nuance can be achieved with a baren and, in some cases, with a flower press.

A print from lace and pin-tucks, with metal hooks from a collar. This was printed on an etching press with oil-based ink and the print was then machine stitched.

MATERIAL	PRINTING PRESS	BURNISHING WITH A SPOON OR BAREN	PRINTING WITH A ROLLER	PRINTING WITH A FLOWER PRESS
carborundum	excellent	good	poor	good
acrylic paste and gel medium	excellent	textures and bumps must be limited; working with fingers and slightly damp paper can give good results	poor	mediocre
plaster	excellent	as above	poor	depends on surface created
thin cardboard	fairly short lifespan, but good	good	good	good
textured paper and wallpaper	variable longevity, according to hardness of paper; details good	good	good if not too textured	good
corrugated cardboard	interesting changing results as squashed	good	good	good
glue	good	good	good	good
PVA glue	good	depends on textures; grains can need a lot of work	mediocre	depends on textures created
string and threads	excellent; can achieve relief and intaglio printing	good as relief print	good as relief print	good
threads and stitching	excellent; longevity variable according to thread type	good	good	good, but thread needs to be very clear
lace (smooth)	good; longevity can be variable	good	mediocre	variable
lace (uneven)	good; longevity can be variable, according to thread type	variable; use fingers as well as baren if necessary	poor	poor
open-weave fabrics	good	variable, according to openness of weave	variable, according to openness of weave	variable
organic materials	often break up under pressure; results can be messy	results easier to control; no break-up	works with very even textures	good
buttons, beads and sequins	can break up under pressure and even cause holes in protection felts	results can be good, according to choice of material	results can be good, according to choice of material	results can be good, according to choice of material
metal parts	ill advised; care must be taken with depth and protection felts	can be successful, according to choice	can be successful, according to choice	can be successful, according to choice
sticky tapes	excellent	good	good	good

How to make a plate

Now we have looked at the choice of materials for the base of the plate and the objects to apply to it, the next step is to put these things together.

Preparation of the plate's surface

Metal and plastic require no particular preparation prior to their use as a base, but other materials may do. Exposed wood, paper, and cardboard surfaces can stick to the printing paper when put through the press, resulting in bits of paper being left behind on the plate and consequently a ruined print. To avoid this, there are various varnishes and stopping agents that can be used as primers.

Ink residues can easily be cleaned off metal and plastic, but not off wood, paper, cork, or cardboard. If these materials are to be cleaned and reused, they will need to be protected, as will the objects added to the plate. Wood and cork can offer interesting textures for the final print, and to preserve these you will need to use a primer, such as a thin acrylic varnish or gesso. Alternatively, apply any appropriate wood varnish on both sides and all edges before starting to create the plate. By doing this thoroughly, and repeating the process if the wood absorbs too much varnish, you will ensure that the base of the plate withstands a long print run and lots of cleaning.

Paper and cardboard can deform not only with the application of glue and ink but also if the varnish, gesso or other medium that is used to protect the objects added to the plate and prevent them sticking to the paper in the press is applied to only one side – this will cause the paper or cardboard to curl up, as will the use of glue. To prevent this, and ensure that the plate will withstand several print runs, it will be necessary to protect both sides of it. This should be done in advance by painting a layer of gesso or acrylic varnish on one side of the paper or card and along the edge, waiting for it to dry, and then painting the other side. Once this has dried, repeat the process. Only now can objects be added to the plate ready for printing. If the intention is to print from such a plate in just one

1. This plate was built up with carpet-quality double-sided tape stuck into place.

2. Blue soft embroidery cotton was then stuck to the tape to create the design.

session until it is exhausted, such protection may be a little academic. In general, I get away with not doing this, especially as I use very little glue, but it can be necessary for some applications and in any case if the plate is to be cleaned after use, it is better to protect both sides.

Applying materials for texture

Once the plate's surface has been prepared, the chosen materials can be added. Remember that whatever design is created on the plate it will be reversed, as in a mirror, when printed, so take this into consideration as you work. A number of methods may be involved here, as follows:

• Textured acrylic mediums can be added with a palette knife or other tool to create a textured flat surface; this may be more uneven if a printing press is to be used.
• Small bits and pieces, threads, grains, cut-out cardboard, and so on can be applied to a ground of PVA glue or strong carpet-quality double-sided tape. Glue should be waterproof to prevent problems if water-based ink is

used. Most types of glue will withstand cleaning with vegetable oil, but not necessarily white spirit, which is the case with PVA glue, for example. Double-sided tape is quick and easy to use, but be aware that the edges of the tape will show in the print, so either they will need to form part of the design or the joins must be covered by the materials that are added to the plate. Double-sided tape can also remain sticky during printing, so be careful to protect any uncovered areas with several coats of gesso, or sprinkle on some carborundum before applying a single coat of gesso.
• To stick metal bits and buttons on, you may need strong contact adhesive or epoxy resin. Follow the instructions carefully and work in a well-ventilated area. If a plate treated with contact adhesive is to be cleaned with white spirit after printing, it will need to be protected with shellac varnish, as glue is soluble in white spirit.
• Bits and pieces can also be stitched down to the surface with hand or machine stitches. This is covered in more detail in Chapter 3.

3. Next, the plate was painted with two coats of gesso.

4. Finally, thickened dye was applied with a sponge brush to make the plate ready to print.

How to protect the plate for printing

Once all the desired objects are attached to the plate, it will need to be protected before printing. This protection must be thorough if the plate is likely to be cleaned and reused. If only one print run is envisaged, the protection does not need to be so thorough, but it is best to give all of the materials at least one coating of some kind of medium so that the plate does not accidentally stick to the paper during printing. The issues to consider are:

• The level of protection required to prevent the paper from sticking to the surface of the plate during printing will depend to a certain extent on the materials used.
• The level and type of protection required if the plate is to be cleaned for a future print run will be determined by whether water-based or solvent-based inks are to be used. For instance, does the plate need to be protected against water infiltration or against the effects of white spirit or a vegetable oil cleaner?
• The creation of marks and textures or the need to preserve white or black areas on the printing plate can be a factor. The way in which ink can be wiped off different protective mediums varies with each one and some can be cleaned more easily than others. That is to say, once the ink has been applied to the plate, it can be wiped or rubbed off some or all of the areas where the textures or materials used do not retain the ink. Ink will remain encrusted in areas of greater texture or on certain surfaces that are more difficult to wipe, such as gesso. This will modulate the colors that are retained, and can be particularly important if printing in only one color. The remaining ink will give nuances of color that are more or less intense.

• The choice of medium will also affect the textures obtained from the objects placed on the plate. If the materials provide good clear textures, this may not be particularly important. If, however, they have more subtle textures, as in the case of some fabrics, stitching, or lace, for example, then a heavy varnish, particularly if applied too generously, can cause loss of detail.

Shellac varnish

This traditional medium, made from insect resin, is often called "button polish" or "French polish." It is very resistant to both white spirit and water, as its solvent is alcohol. To ensure that a plate will last for a greater number of prints, apply two coats of shellac varnish to both sides of it, allowing 24–48 hours of drying time between each coat.

Gesso

If gesso is applied sparingly, it will dry in an hour or two and protect the plate so that the paper will not stick to it. If double-sided tape has been used on the plate, two coats of gesso will be necessary. Apply each coat thinly to avoid loss of detail, and for quick drying, but make sure that all areas, even the textured areas that are most difficult to get into, are thoroughly sealed. If the gesso is applied unevenly, it will change the texture of the plate; although this may provide interest in the final print, it

Olive Trees. The silk crepe and acrylic paste trees were protected with gesso before being printed with oil-based ink on an etching press.

River Bank. The plate was made with acrylic gel medium, with silk and fabric waste protected with acrylic varnish.

Acrylic medium

There are various acrylic mediums. Though these vary, they all tend to provide a surface that can be wiped quite cleanly, and so give a very different result from gesso. Gloss medium is particularly useful; matt medium retains some ink. These mediums protect the plate's surface better than gesso, so a few more prints may be achieved.

Acrylic varnish

This is a water-based varnish that makes it easy to clean materials and brushes, gives better protection than acrylic medium and gesso, and allows ink to be wiped off easily if this is required. Apply two coats on both sides of the plate for good-quality protection. Its life expectancy is better than acrylic medium and gesso, but not as good as shellac varnish. However, its drying time is much shorter, and it is less expensive. Many acrylic manufacturers produce an acrylic medium and varnish combined – experiment with whatever is available.

Marine varnish

Quality varnishes such as marine varnish will extend the life of a plate and are useful if you are working on a wood-based surface. Apply two very thin coats for good protection without losing too much texture and detail. However, be aware that varnishes do affect how the plate is wiped clean: once varnished, the whole plate will be wiped in the same way, which may not be desirable. With all varnishes, work in a well-ventilated area, wear protective gloves and wash all brushes thoroughly.

means that the plate will dry unevenly. It is important to make sure that the plate is completely dry before printing – any lumps of gesso that are not dry when the plate is printed will squash and leave white marks on the print. In order to get an even, all-over coverage, I use a stiff brush to apply the gesso thoroughly onto the plate and into all the difficult textural areas, and then, where necessary, wipe off any excess with the same stiff brush.

Gesso will retain a certain amount of ink, even when wiped clean with a cloth. The only way to remove any ink in areas that you do not wish to print is with the appropriate solvent – that is, water, oil, or white spirit.

For plates printed with water-based ink the surface of the plate can be quickly cleaned with a damp rag or kitchen paper after use. When using oil-based ink the plate can be given a light clean with a rag or toothbrush, using vegetable oil or white spirit. Repeated cleaning will shorten the life of delicate plates.

Planning ahead

When making the plate it is best to consider beforehand how you intend the print to look, how the print is to be made, and what media are to be used, as different types of plate react better or less well to different printing techniques. Experimentation with different techniques will help you to identify the best methods.

CHAPTER 2

MEDIA AND SURFACES FOR PRINT

Practical aspects to consider

Every artist has their favorite media, and this applies in printing too. Before deciding which inks and media you wish to use there are quite a few practical aspects that have to be considered. The following sections look at some of the things that you will need to think about.

Cost and availability

To begin with you may wish to invest very little while you try things out, but as you move on you may want to use more appropriate specialized media, which will be more expensive. The cheapest materials to use, as they require no investment, are those that you already possess! Most textile artists will have acrylic paints at home, and perhaps also some dyes. If this applies to you, why not try out these media for your first attempts? They are great for relief printing and will work satisfactorily for intaglio printing. They also work well if printing by hand with a spoon, baren or roller, as is likely when you first start.

Acrylic paints are widely available from artists' materials shops and items such as homemade retarders are easy to obtain. All of the other products mentioned in this chapter are easily accessible through the Internet (see Suppliers, page 127).

Wood. This was printed with thickened dye on calico that had previously been printed with a monoprint. It was embellished with free-motion machine embroidery, using feather stitch and whip stitch.

Snow in the Marshes. The colors were developed over a series of prints from this plate, made with stitch, fabric, and acrylic paste. It was printed with oil-based ink on an etching press.

Drying time

The drying times of different media vary, but an extended drying time is desirable for several reasons:

- The time taken from inking up the plate to printing it can be a few minutes or perhaps even up to an hour if the plate is big, or if different areas have to be carefully inked in different colors. During this time the medium used must stay wet.
- If the print is to be printed with a press, this won't take very long, but if it is being hand printed using a spoon or baren, the process will be much longer. Again, the medium used must stay wet during the whole time.
- Interesting results can often be achieved by adding extra colors to a plate on which the residue of a previous color remains; by carefully choosing the colors used, you can obtain intriguing crossovers. To exploit this process a slow drying time is required.
- When using a press the ink can be rubbed into the crevices for an intaglio print and then another color of ink can be rolled on for printing in relief. During the time taken to do this, the medium or ink must stay wet.

Oil-based ink has a very long drying time: if any ink is left on a plate, there will still be a residual amount if printed the following day. The new water-washable oil-based ink also has an extended drying time, making it as easy to use as the original oil-based ink. The drying times of other media can be extended with various products, as suggested later in the chapter.

Ease of use

It is important to establish how easy the medium is to apply to the plate, and how easy it is to clean afterwards. Acrylic-based products are much more malleable than oil-based ink. Water-washable ink, which was essentially created for intaglio printing, is also easier to apply than oil-based ink, although additives exist for both oil-based and water-washable inks that improve their application and their ability to be wiped successfully.

It is undeniable that being able to clean everything with soap and water is much easier than using any solvents. Water-washable etching ink and all acrylic media can be simply cleaned in water and, if necessary, a little washing-up liquid. Acrylic media must not be allowed to dry on the materials and brushes, so these should be cleaned regularly during a print session and rapidly once the printing has been finished. If, however, your brushes have been ruined with dried-on acrylic or PVA glue, they can generally be restored with The Masters Brush Cleaner and Preserver – soap them really well and leave them for up to half an hour, and even the most hardened brushes can come back to life.

Cleaning and toxicity of oil-based ink

Traditionally, oil-based ink is cleaned up with white spirit (mineral spirits), but although this has low acute toxicity, continued exposure by inhalation or to the skin can lead to severe health problems. If you use white spirit, do so in a well ventilated area and wear gloves, and for environmental reasons it is best not to dispose of white spirit directly into the drainage system. For artists working constantly with oil-based ink who may find that this is not sufficient protection, other methods of cleaning up exist.

There are various natural citrus-based products on the market that can be used as an alternative to white spirit, but in general these are very expensive. Two excellent non-toxic products for cleaning all oil-based ink are cheap vegetable oil (most will work; I use sunflower oil) and washing-up liquid (I use an ecologically sound citrus-based one, which is excellent). Mix the detergent with water and keep it in a spray bottle for ease of use.

To clean all equipment, wipe off as much ink as possible with kitchen towel or old newspaper, then pour on a little vegetable oil using an old squeegee bottle. The oil will gradually dissolve and thin the ink so that it can be removed more easily with the kitchen towel or similar. If the ink has been on the mixing plate for a while, leave the oil for up to 15 minutes to thin it down. Wipe off the dissolved ink, spray with detergent and wipe again. Repeat the process if necessary. The collagraphy plate can also be cleaned with vegetable oil – rub in a small amount with your fingers or an old toothbrush, leave it

for about 15 minutes, and then wipe it clean, finishing it off with a spray from the detergent bottle. Kitchen towel used in the cleaning process can also be used to clean brushes, rollers and the inking slab. Hands can be cleaned with vegetable oil, followed by washing-up liquid. In practice, I find oil just as easy to use as white spirit, and much more agreeable.

For thorough cleaning where the ink has dried on a little, use a small amount of citrus cleaner or Vegetable Cleaning Agent (VCA) to finish it off. This is not volatile and so doesn't pose any health risk, but it isn't kind to hands, so wear gloves. However, with careful use of ink this shouldn't be necessary in the first place – I always manage to clean with vegetable oil. If you are leaving ink on the slab for any length of time, or for use the next day, cover it with clingfilm to preserve its freshness.

Printing by hand or with a press

The choice of medium to be used can depend on whether the print is to be printed by hand or with a press. For instance, I have found that hand printing is more successful if larger quantities of ink or other media are applied to the plate. This would not be acceptable if using oil-based ink, which tends to be unpleasant if printed too thickly, and so for this reason I prefer acrylic-based media or thickened dye for hand printing.

Surfaces for printing

The type of surface that is to be used for the print, whether textile or paper, and its quality can also affect the choice of medium. Although acrylic paint and both oil-based and Aqua Wash inks give good results on fabric, it may be preferable to use adapted media if the fabric is to be washed repeatedly. In this case, choose acrylic paint and fabric medium, or dye made up to the recipe given on page 44. However, inks tend to create a finer image, so this should be a consideration if the fabric is not going to be washed. All media work well on paper, but will give different results according to their drying time and viscosity.

Different media for printing

Being aware of some of the practical aspects relating to the different media will help to inform the choice of media for printing. The following sections look at the various options that are available.

Acrylic paint

Acrylic paint is ideal for simple hand printing, but the disadvantage of this medium is its quick drying time. If the paint is simply rolled onto the plate and printed quickly, this may not be too problematic, although cleaning up afterwards will be. However, in order to have enough time to vary the colors across the plate it will be necessary to extend the drying time. To achieve this, most acrylic paint manufacturers offer at least one retarder, which can be added to the paint to lengthen its drying time. Follow the instructions and don't add too much retarder, or the paint will not dry at all.

For a cheaper and more readily available option, try a few drops of washing-up liquid. Although this does not extend the drying time of acrylics as much as the commercial mediums, it can be enough. Glycerine alcohol, available as a food additive, is a component of acrylic retarders and so will also do the trick. Use five parts water to one part glycerine and put a few drops into the paint. Be aware, however, that though this additive works with fine layers of acrylic paint on paper (and therefore will work for printing), it can be problematic where thickly applied paint may take a long time to dry and be affected by subsequent layers – the same types of mixing and blending problems can occur as when oil paint is badly applied.

Clean up acrylic paint with water, and washing-up liquid if necessary, immediately after use. Never let acrylics dry on your work materials.

Wood detail. The textures were created with plaster and carborundum on a cardboard plate. It was printed with acrylic paint on 40gsm Japanese paper, using a baren.

Acrylic paint and fabric medium

If printing a collagraphy plate onto fabric, these products offer a fairly simple solution to a problem: mixing acrylic paint with a fabric medium will enable the paint to adhere to and penetrate the fabric more easily. The fabric medium gives a softer result on the fabric print than acrylic paint alone. Two fabric medium products are fairly widely available: Liquitex Fabric Medium and GAC 900 medium from Golden Artist Colors Inc. These mediums can be heat-fixed after application to withstand washing.

To use these products:

1. Wash the fabric first to eliminate any fabric size – a little bicarbonate of soda added to the washing water will help this.

2. Mix the fabric medium with a soft-bodied acrylic paint – don't use the heavy-bodied variety of acrylic paint for this method. The recommended mix is one part fabric medium to one part acrylic paint.

3. The drying time is improved by the addition of the fabric medium, which is used for silk-screen printing where an extended drying time is essential, so no other additive is required.

4. Fix the print once it has dried. This must be done in a well-ventilated area as the dye paint releases low levels of formaldehyde during setting. Setting can be done by ironing for several minutes on the reverse side of the fabric with a hot iron without steam. Move over a fairly small area at a time so that the work stays hot for at least three minutes. If the chosen fabric won't accept a hot iron, use a medium temperature but iron for longer. The paint can also be heat set in an oven at 250°F (120°C) for four minutes or 300°F (150°C) for one to two minutes.

5. It is recommended that the item should not be washed for a further three or four days to allow for complete curing.

6. Any leftover fabric paint can be stored in an airtight container for future use.

Acrylic paint was mixed with equal quantities of fabric medium to print from a stitched plate with open-weave fabric and acrylic paste. It was printed with a baren and fingers on calico.

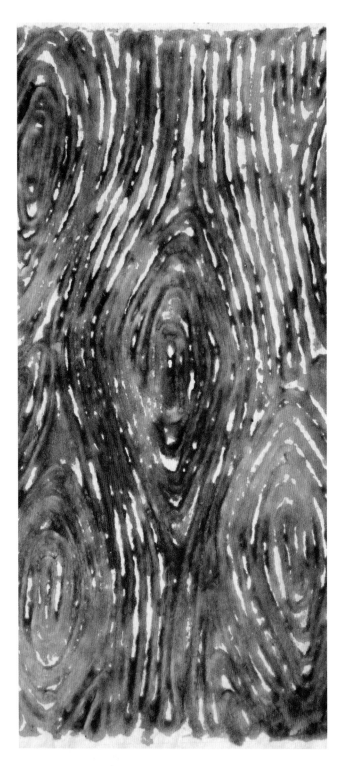

Wood detail. This was printed with acrylic ink onto very damp 40gsm Japanese paper with a flower press.

Acrylic ink

Acrylic ink is useful for lino printing. The major problem with all things acrylic, as we have seen, is their drying time, which can be pretty rapid unless slowed down with special mediums (see pages 40–41) or even a few drops of washing-up liquid. This means that developing multiple colors on the plate, as with oil-based and water-washable inks (see page 44), is a little difficult to achieve. However, the drying time of acrylic ink is perfectly acceptable for most applications without an additive.

I haven't found these inks particularly useful for printing with a press, where thin layers of slow-drying ink allow for interesting effects when using intaglio and relief printing at the same time. They are very useful for hand-printing methods, though, as largish quantities of ink can be applied to the plate (see pages 88–91).

As with acrylic paint, clean up with water, and washing-up liquid if necessary, immediately after use. Never let acrylic media dry on your work materials.

Oil-based ink

Oil-based ink gives fine-quality results and its very slow drying time allows for colors to be mixed on the plate, and for an intaglio and a relief print to be created at the same time from the same plate. It should be applied thinly for best results, so do be careful to roll the ink out really well if using a roller, or use small amounts on a brush or dolly (see pages 88–91). Special easy-wipe compounds exist to enable this ink to be spread more easily into the crevices of a collagraph plate and to be wiped afterwards if required. Oil-based ink gives good, fast results on fabric, although it may wear with repeated heavy washing. As already mentioned, cleaning up is more of a problem with this ink – see page 39 for environmentally and user-friendly cleaning techniques.

Although oil-based ink does contain a solvent, this is volatile at only a very slow rate and, therefore, is not considered to pose health problems in normal use. Nevertheless, many artists now refuse to use oil-based ink altogether since the advent of water-washable substitutes.

Blue Rags. The colors were developed over a series of prints from this plate, made with fabric and acrylic paste. It was printed with oil-based ink on an etching press.

Water-washable ink

The new water-washable etching ink is made with an oil emulsion that allows for similar work and results as traditional oil-based ink. It can be used in all printing techniques. It does not contain water and must be diluted with its own special oil or easy-wipe compound – there is one for colors and one especially for black to allow it to keep its intensity. The ink has the same drying time as traditional oil-based ink, but is odorless, light-fast, non-toxic, and permanent when dry. It cleans up with soap and water. The major suppliers of this new ink are Charbonnel (Aqua Wash), who also produce an oil-based ink, Caligo (Safe Wash), and Rostow & Jung (Akua Intaglio – water-based and non-toxic).

Most of the colors can be wiped more easily than their oil-based cousins, so if you wipe some of the ink off the plate before printing, be careful not to overdo it. The prepared damp paper for this ink should also be a little less damp than it would be for oil-based ink. A further advantage of this ink is that the tarlatan rags and dollies used for application and wiping can be washed and reused – although these rags could also be used to add color and textural interest to embroideries once dry!

Dye

Dye is quite different from fabric paint because it actually bonds with the molecules of the fabric, rather than sitting on the surface. The fabric is therefore completely soft after washing, whereas a fabric paint will give a different feel to the fabric, more or less stiff according to the quality of the paint. Most bought fabric paints have drying times that are just too short for printing, but fabric paint can be made with acrylic paint and fabric medium (see page 41). Screen-printing inks for fabrics may be a suitable solution for certain collagraphic plates as their drying time is necessarily longer for this technique, but dyes are generally a better option as they stay wet for longer.

Good results can be obtained by making thickened dye using the following recipe. This option is also by far the most economical in the long term. The urea in this recipe keeps up the level of humidity in the dye, allowing time for it to strike on the fabric. In hot dry conditions the amount can be increased to 140g (5oz) per litre (1¾ pints).

You will need:
- 100g (3½oz) urea
- 1 tsp Calgon or Metaphos
- 375ml (13fl oz) hot water
- 20g (¾oz) soda ash (if the fabric has not been prepared in advance – see below for how to do this)
- 35g (1¼oz) Manutex RS or Jacquard Sodium Alginate SH *or* 70g (2½oz) Manutex F700 or Jacquard Sodium Alginate F, which is better for fine lines
- 575ml (19fl oz) cool water

Method:
1. Mix the urea and Calgon into the hot water until dissolved. If required, add the 20g (¾oz) soda ash at this stage.
2. Add the Manutex RS (or F700 if using) with an electric beater if possible to prevent lumps forming.
3. Slowly pour in the cool water and mix thoroughly.

For every 125ml (4fl oz) of thickener used you will require ½–2 tsp of Procion MX dye powder, according to the color and intensity desired. If soda ash has been mixed into the dye thickener, the dye will be usable for only about four hours. For this reason it may be better to soak the fabric in soda ash solution beforehand. If the thickened dye does not contain soda ash, any left over can be stored in a cool place for up to a week. Whether or not soda ash has been added to the dye thickener, the thickener can be stored in a fridge for four to six weeks without any dye in it and used as required. Be sure to label the container carefully and clearly.

To soak the fabric beforehand, use one of the following recipes:

You will need:
• 200g (7oz) washing soda
• 1 litre (1¾ pints) hot water
or
• 20g (¾oz) soda ash
• 1 litre (1¾ pints) hot water

Method:
1. In both cases, dissolve the powder in the hot water.
2. Soak the fabric for about 40 minutes.

This solution can be kept in a jar (carefully labeled) and reused whenever required. For printing, allow the soaked fabric to dry naturally (not in a dryer), then iron to take out the creases. Use an old iron, or protect it with an old cloth, otherwise a white powder will be left on the iron's surface. Be careful when ironing as the prepared fabric scorches easily. The fabric is now ready to dye.

Using dye on fabric

The dyes can be applied to the plate with a roller or a sponge paintbrush. The print can then be batched to fix the dye in the usual way – that is, wrapped in a plastic bag to keep it damp and left in a warm place at above 73°F (23°C) for six hours or overnight. For a large print, roll it up in plastic so that the printed areas do not touch each other. To improve the strike, it can be ironed for five minutes once dry or placed in an oven for five minutes at 300°F (150°C).

Rinse the fabric in cold water until it runs clear and then in very hot water to release any remaining dye. At this stage, add 2ml (0.07fl oz) of Synthrapol or Metapex 38 to 1 liter (1¾ pints) of hot water to prevent any excess dye leaching out and staining the white areas of the print. Leave the fabric immersed for about 20 minutes. Rinse again in cold water and leave to dry naturally.

The resulting fabric will retain its original handling quality, which is an advantage over all the other techniques and media. Given the extra work involved, perhaps this process is really only worth it if good fabric fall and handling are necessary for the final piece, but for those artists who already have a collection of dyes this can be a very economical way of printing. The natural quality of the fabric that results from dyeing can also help with the choice of embellishment techniques, particularly if you are using an Embellisher machine, where a stiffer, inked fabric may be more difficult to work with. Please note that this dyeing technique is for natural fibers only.

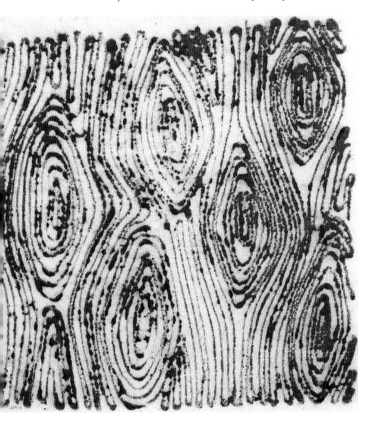

Wood. This design was printed with thickened dye on calico with a roller.

Inks or dyes?

With inks it is possible to print on any type of fabric, including synthetics. If using dyes or paint dyes, the choice will be limited to the types of fabric that the dye will work on: with Procion MX dyes, for example, natural fabrics such as cotton, linen, silk, and rayon can be used. Finely woven textiles will produce fine details from a plate, whereas coarse linen or raw silk will give less detailed results but perhaps interesting textures, which can lead to another area of experimentation. Remember to leave enough fabric around the print area to allow for manipulation under the sewing machine, or to place the work in an embroidery hoop if necessary.

Printing and cleaning

Depending on the protection given to the plate and the materials that have been used on it, an average of between ten and twenty prints should be feasible. This means that with one plate it is possible to try out different media on different surfaces, as well as different color combinations. Remember, if working with both water-based and oil-based media, to use the water-based medium first, clean and dry the plate, and then use the oil-based medium.

The plate can be cleaned for reuse according to the medium used. A toothbrush can be useful for cleaning difficult areas. The plate can then be dried naturally and stored for further use. If the plate is exhausted – that is, too flattened to provide further prints – then cleaning it is academic. In fact, the colored plate may be lovely in its own right and another use could be envisaged for it, such as including it in embroidery or paper work, for example.

For many of the experiments in this book, I printed by hand first to take full advantage of the plate before it was subsequently flattened by a press. On the other hand, some of the plates were just too uneven for hand printing, so the press helped to even them out before I printed them by hand. If you have easy access to a press, there really isn't much point in using hand-printing

methods except for very delicate surfaces. If, however, only occasional access to a press is possible – for example, through day schools and classes or at a friend's home – it can be worth using the two methods in tandem. Printing a plate by hand in advance can help to stimulate ideas about how to exploit it when a press becomes available.

Papers for printing

Just as artists have their favorite media for printing, they also have their favorite papers. There are various aspects to consider when choosing paper – you can't just use a piece torn out of a sketchbook! For etching, and even more so for collagraphy printing, the demands on the paper are very specific. It has to mold around the shape of the plate and the materials attached to it, preferably without tearing or creasing. The paper therefore needs to be extremely malleable, and this means that it must have long fibers. The thickness of the paper required, however, will depend on the method of printing chosen.

There are essentially three different types of printing – relief printing with a roller, hand printing with a baren or spoon, and printing with a press – and each will place different demands on the paper.

Relief printing with a roller is much like lino printing. If the paper is very thick, more pressure will be required on the roller, so try medium papers around 200gsm. However, fine Japanese-style papers that are suitable for woodblock printing are great for this technique.

Printing with a baren or spoon is the technique most similar to woodblock printing. For this reason, choose similar types of paper to those used for this method – fine, tough Japanese-style mulberry papers are ideal. It is a good idea to have some newsprint available to try out the print first before using these expensive papers.

Spread the paper onto the plate with a baren and then gradually work all over it. It can be useful to dampen the paper before printing, although this can make it less resistant to the baren. One way round this is to use just slightly damp paper and place some tissue paper on top of this to protect it from any excessive rubbing. To dampen fine paper, put it in a tray of water for just a couple of seconds, remove it and then blot it. Hang it up and allow it to dry a little – it should remain ever so slightly damp. The dampened paper will pick up acrylic ink better and will be more malleable if the plate is not very flat.

When printing with a press, good results can be obtained on many different types of paper, including craft paper, home-made gummy silk paper, watercolor paper, and any of the Japanese papers used for woodblock printing, although very fine ones may break under the press if the plate is rough or very uneven. There are also many papers on the market that are specifically for printing etchings with a press, and these are ideal for collagraphy too. The most important characteristic of these papers is their malleability, which is due to a long fiber length. Without these long fibers they would tear over the textures and reliefs of a plate, particularly when printing on a press with its heavy roller and increased pressure. They have less size too, so they pick up the inks more easily.

The textures of watercolor paper stay on the plate if it is not cleaned between prints, so use a smooth paper if you are working on a long print run where complex colors are being developed. The paper I generally use is a 300gsm commercially produced etching paper.

Venetian House. The plate was made by drawing into wet plaster on cardboard. It was first printed onto linen sheeting before being printed onto etching paper. The weave of the linen is still visible in areas of the print.

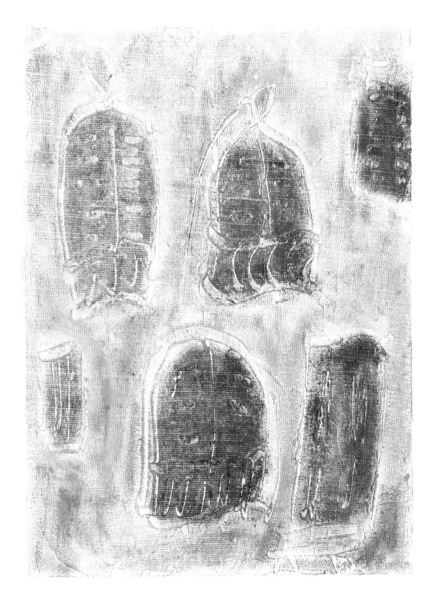

Papers for printing with a flower press

Fine papers are better for this technique as the printing pressure is not as great as with a traditional press. The result will be better still if the paper has been dampened first, as explained on page 47.

Preparing paper for printing

For the best results all papers (with the exception of home-made gummy silk paper and craft paper) are soaked prior to printing for up to fifteen minutes and then hung up to dry – they are ready for printing when they are barely damp. This process makes the fibers even more malleable, which means that the print is better and the paper is less likely to crease or tear. For convenience I prepare several sheets of paper for a printing session, and when they are just slightly damp I put them in a plastic bag ready for use. The paper can be kept in this way for a day or two. If it is not all used, allow it to dry – it can be soaked again for another session and will be fine as long as this process is not repeated too often.

Paper soaking in a tray.

Paper hanging up to dry before being put in a plastic bag ready for printing.

Altering papers

Once confidence in using certain media and techniques has been built up, the next step could be experimenting with your chosen papers. For example, they can be collaged together either before printing or during the printing process. The papers could be torn or cut for different areas of the print, bringing more colors and perhaps textural interest into the final print. Do be careful in your choice of papers, however, as some decorative ones are not light-resistant and will fade over time.

Collaging techniques

For relief printing with a roller or baren it may be more prudent to collage the papers together beforehand to make sure that they are thoroughly stuck down, as the roller or baren may not go over the whole of the paper surface. Use a suitable malleable cornflour paste (see right) to make the collage, and a roller or several books to ensure good adhesion. Be careful that the resulting paper does not become too thick to create a useful print. Leave the paper to dry before using it to print.

Chine-collé. The plate has been inked ready for printing and strips of fine 10gsm iris paper, with cornstarch glue applied to their top surfaces, have been put into position. This is now ready for the etching paper to be placed on top, before being passed through the etching press.

When printing with a press it is usual to collage the papers together at the time of printing, generally applying an interesting fine paper to a firmer support. This technique is called *chine-collé*. Using different papers in this way can bring color, life, and texture to a print. It is traditionally done with cornstarch glue: PVA glue can also be used, but I find the cornstarch glue much easier.

To make cornstarch glue:
1. Add 1 teaspoon of cornstarch to 2 tbsp (30 ml) water in a small saucepan.
2. Stir to a cream and then add another 2 tbsp (30 ml) of water.
3. Stir over the heat until the mixture thickens to a thin custard consistency.

The mixture needs to stay warm in a flask or it may become lumpy, so it is best to make only small usable batches at a time. Keep the flask closed when not in use. The above quantity will be enough to glue about six pieces measuring 6" × 6" (15 × 15 cm), so it can be very quickly used up and should not go lumpy in that time.

If this mixture is thinned down further, it can be used for sizing handmade paper. If made a little thicker, it can be used for attaching prints to a surface when framing, as it is considered to be of archival quality.

To make a print using the *chine-collé* technique:
1. Dampen the paper or papers in the usual way. For convenience, they can simply be dampened with a sponge and then blotted to remove excess water.
2. Cut or tear out different shapes and visualize their position on the plate before inking up the plate for use.
3. Paste the papers on one side with cornstarch or PVA glue and arrange them on top of the inked plate, which should already be in place on the press. Ensure that the glued side of the papers is uppermost.
4. Put the prepared damp etching paper on top of the plate where the papers are already in place. The

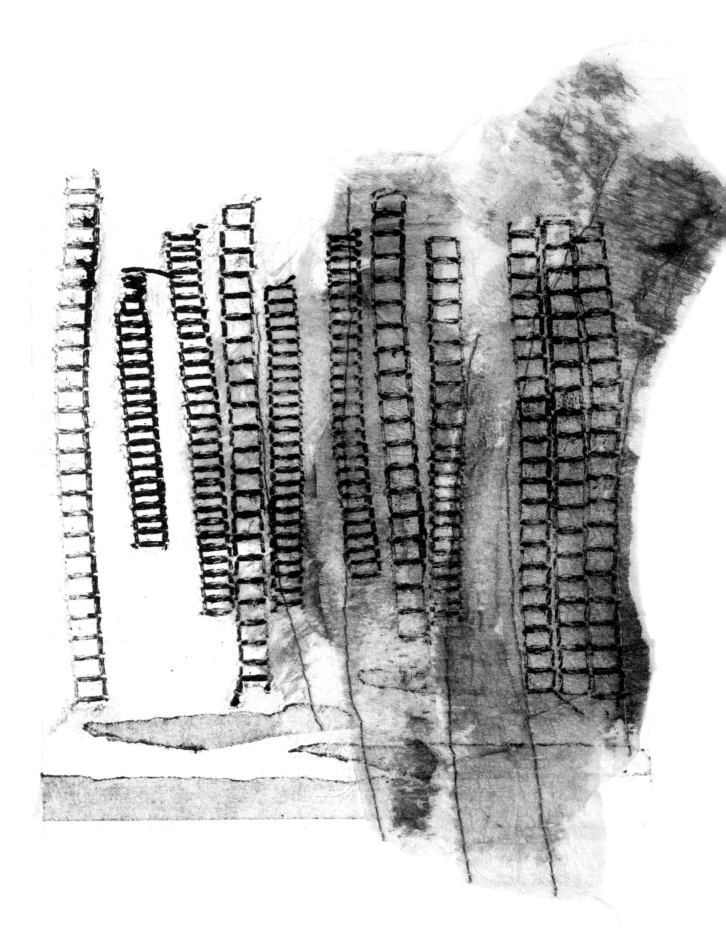

chine-collé papers will adhere to the ink on the plate well enough to remain undisturbed when the etching paper is positioned.

5. Put the felts in place as usual and run the print through the press. The ink from the plate will print onto the *chine-collé* papers and any of the etching paper that is visible, and the pressure from the press will laminate all the papers together.

Adding machine stitching

Another interesting way of altering papers if you are using a press, or even for some printing in relief, is to collage papers together with machine stitching. Simple appliqué using straight lines or zigzag stitching can add interest to the final print. More all-over stitching can also animate the surface, although this may undermine the strength of the paper. This raises a dilemma: on one hand the stitching on the paper can reinforce the collaged areas, but on the other it can weaken the paper if there are areas of holes close together. If the embroidered paper tears during printing, this will be due to a weakening of the paper as a result of too much stitching. But does this really matter? The resulting print could be stitched back together or used with other textile media.

This method of preparing paper is less suitable for hand printing, where the reduced pressure available may not enable a good print to be taken around the stitched areas. However, given the amount of interest that the stitching and collage can add to the paper, this may not always be a problem.

Urban Landscape.
Paper made from silk rod waste (a by-product of silk production) was prepared and colored with drawing ink. It was then stitched with free-motion embroidery to etching paper. This was printed with water-washable ink under a press, using the same plate as *Urban Landscape* on page 13.

Fossil II. This shows the iris paper printed and glued to the etching paper at the same time, using the *chine-collé* technique.

Fabrics for printing

For good quality prints on fabric it is best to choose fabrics with a high thread count: the more open or coarse the fibers, the less well the design reads. Having said this, you can get interesting results using a highly textured plate on textured fabric. For fine line work and detail, however, fine fabrics with a high thread count will be essential. Fine linen, calico, or silk will work very well. For coarser work old linen sheets can be interesting, but the printed fibers tend to show up more than the design, making further embroidery work almost essential.

Fabrics for relief printing with a roller

If printing on fabrics, use something stiff but smooth, such as a firm calico, or the fabric could move into the relief areas and the print could become distorted. Another solution is to use the collagraphy plate as a stamp. Place the fabric on the table and put a couple of cloths underneath it to provide a slightly soft base. Place the inked plate face downwards onto the fabric and roll over it to press it down firmly. Continue in this way until a satisfactory result is achieved. You could try using this method for printing more difficult or finer fabrics.

Fabrics for hand printing with a baren or spoon

For printing on fabrics, choose fine, firm fabrics, such as calico, to avoid distorting the final print. Spread the fabric out onto the plate with a baren and then start burnishing all over. Another way to keep the fabric in the right place while printing with a baren is to fix it with drawing pins to the work station, with the plate underneath it, and then start the burnishing.

Fabrics for printing with a press

Any fabric is worth trying on a printing press. Plain fabrics will react differently depending on their qualities and textures. Pre-dyed fabrics and commercially printed ones might also make interesting starting points. Be aware, however, that the ink can seep through fabric when it is put under so much pressure, so protect the felts of the printing press with more fabric or craft paper to prevent them being printed too! Thickened dyes can also work well in a press; again, protect the felts with extra layers of fabric or paper.

Fossil. Homemade gummy silk paper made from cocoon strippings can work well if it is relatively fine. Use a spoon and fingers so as not to move the paper around too much. The print was layered with another piece of colored gummy silk paper and stitched to a mitsumata pulp paper.

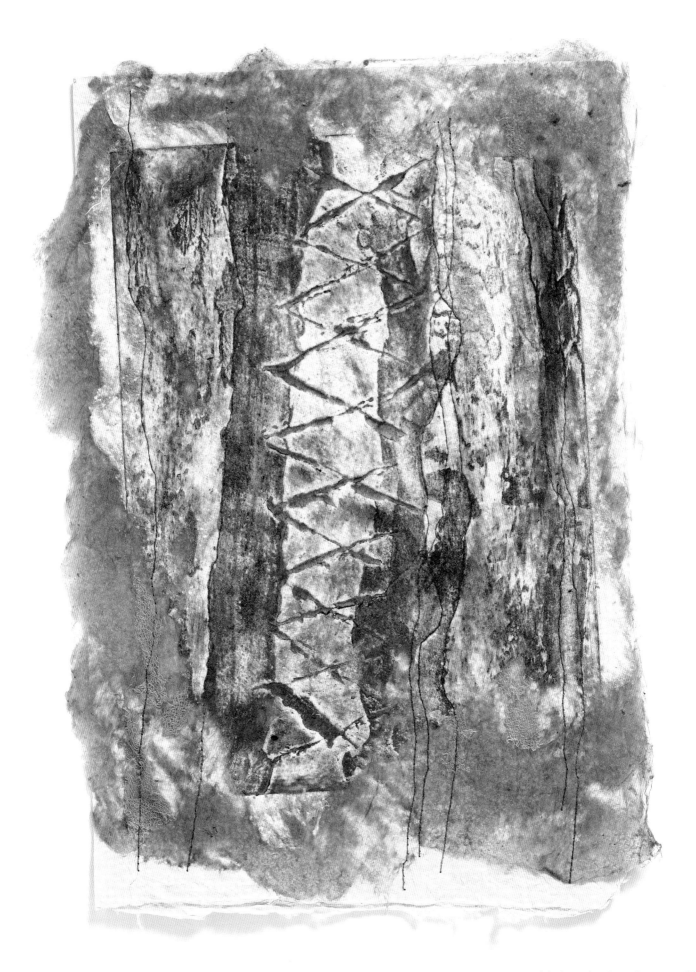

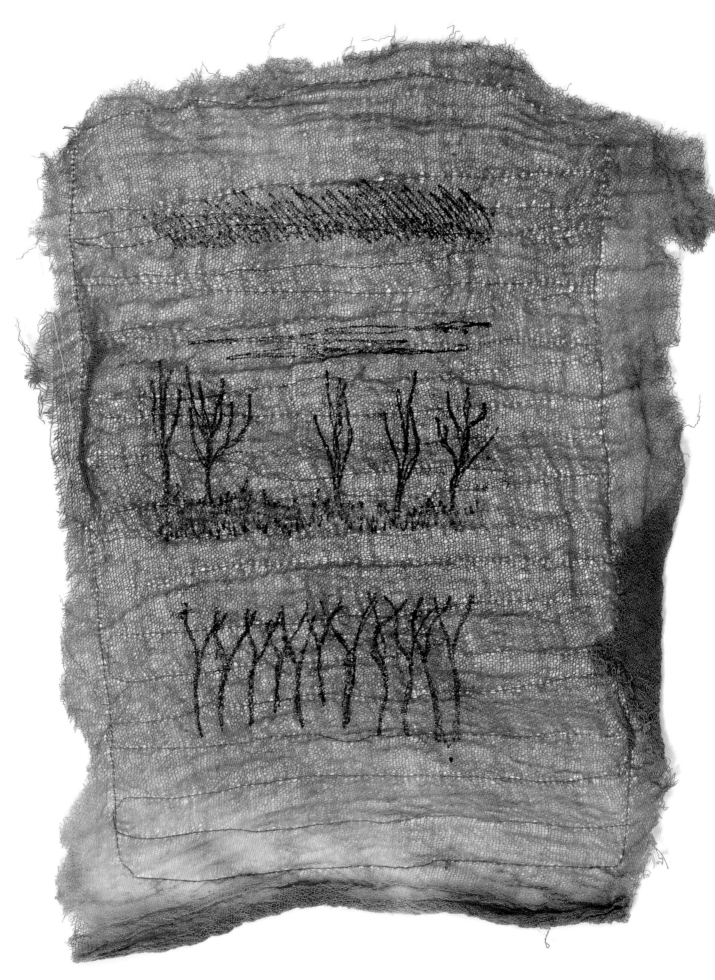

Altering fabrics

Fabrics can also be developed before printing with a collagraph plate. For your first attempts at collagraphy on fabric, using calico is a good idea because of its firm quality; alternatively, use old linen sheets. Taking a piece of fabric that is already colored or printed can also provide a good starting point for creating an image with depth and more interest. Try a bought piece of fabric or a recycled piece that has interesting colors and marks that relate to an idea you have developed in a plate for printing.

Adding color

For a more complicated piece the fabric could be developed beforehand, using dyeing methods such as wax resist, tie dye or discharge techniques. Make sure that the fabric remains supple enough to print on. The themes and colors developed on the fabric should have resonance with the plate and the ink or dye colors chosen. The position of the print on the fabric could even be determined by the way in which the fabric is developed. Multiple layering of images can create truly complex effects.

Late Autumn in the Vines.
Dyed cotton scrim was stitched to etching paper for printing. The plate was made by stitching on plastic with thick sewing cotton.

Adding stitch

Fabrics can be stitched, collaged, or patched together before being printed. The marks made by the stitching or patching will be seen through the inked image – how much will depend on the image and the amount of color applied. The result could be very subtle, with the marked or embroidered fabric submerged under the ink and color, or the patching and stitching could become an important part of the finished image. Here are a few ideas:

• Try using different colors of material patched together, or different textures in similar colors.
• Fabrics could be stitched together using careful seaming by machine.
• Use free-motion embroidery to stitch all over a collection of different fabrics before printing.
• Hand stitches holding the patched fabrics together could be interesting – try small delicate stitches or big clumsy stitches of the sort you would use to repair the holes in a patched fabric.

If the fabric created becomes too hard and stiff, it may be difficult to print with anything other than a press, although a relief print with a baren should be possible as long as the altered fabric is relatively uniform in depth. Thickened dye works well with relief printing, so this could be the best choice of medium. If the fabric created is very uneven in depth, this too could cause a problem under a press, but adding more or softer blankets on top of the fabric and plate before printing will help with this.

Interesting surfaces can be created for printing by collaging the materials first, but the resulting print could become too disjointed or even difficult to produce if the print method is not adapted. Experimentation with all of these methods will be the key to success in knowing just how far you can go with collaging and altering the surface for print, depending on the hand or printing-press technique that you intend to use.

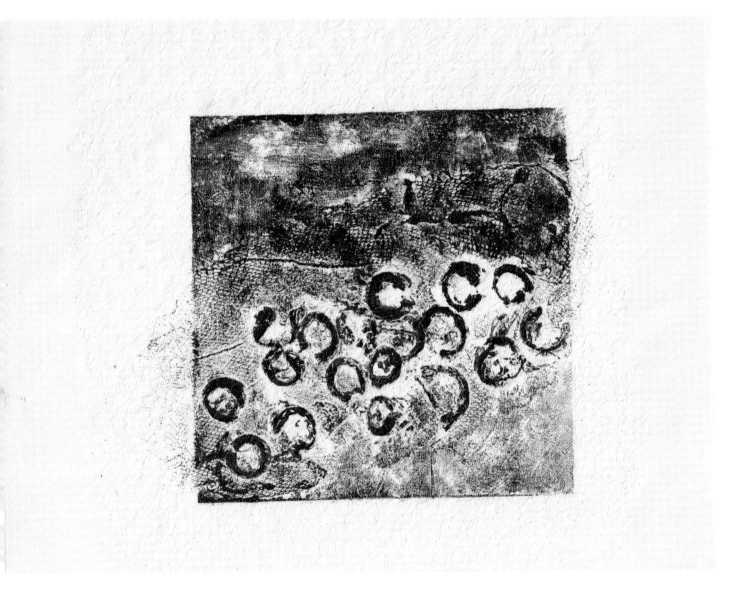

Venice. Hand-patched fabrics with very visible stitching in rich cloth form the base for this print. The richness of Venice is evoked, but with the notion that it is held together by a thread. The plate was made by stitching on plastic with thick sewing thread.

Urban Landscape. The cotton fabric used as a starting point was stitched all over with zigzag stitching to add extra texture before being printed.

CHAPTER ‹ 3 ›
INTRODUCING BRODAGRAPHY

Using embroidery and textile techniques

The materials for applying to the plate covered in Chapter 1 are fairly classic in collagraphy. In this chapter we look at the different surfaces and textures that can be achieved by including embroidery in the construction of the plate. This is what I mean by the term *brodagraphy*. Fabric manipulation with stitch or heat can also produce interesting surface textures. Many of the prints shown in previous chapters include stitching, so now it's time to take a closer look at this technique.

I particularly like to involve embroidery and textile techniques in the construction of my plates for printing as this creates a very potent relationship between my textile work and the print side of my art practice. Stitching and stitch marks can be very expressive with reference to garment making, traditional embroidery and textile techniques, and can therefore carry a wide cultural relevance. Stitched line, stitch marks, and fabric manipulation may also be useful simply for the textural qualities that they can bring to a plate.

Vague écriture. A free-motion straight stitch was applied to a card plate, followed by a cable stitch worked from the back with soft embroidery cotton. The plate was inked with a dolly, then printed (print not shown). The color left in the crevices was allowed to remain and only the threads were inked again with a roller for a second print. As a result, the relief areas are a stronger color and the crevices of the plate are visible as a paler blue. The plate was printed on an etching press.

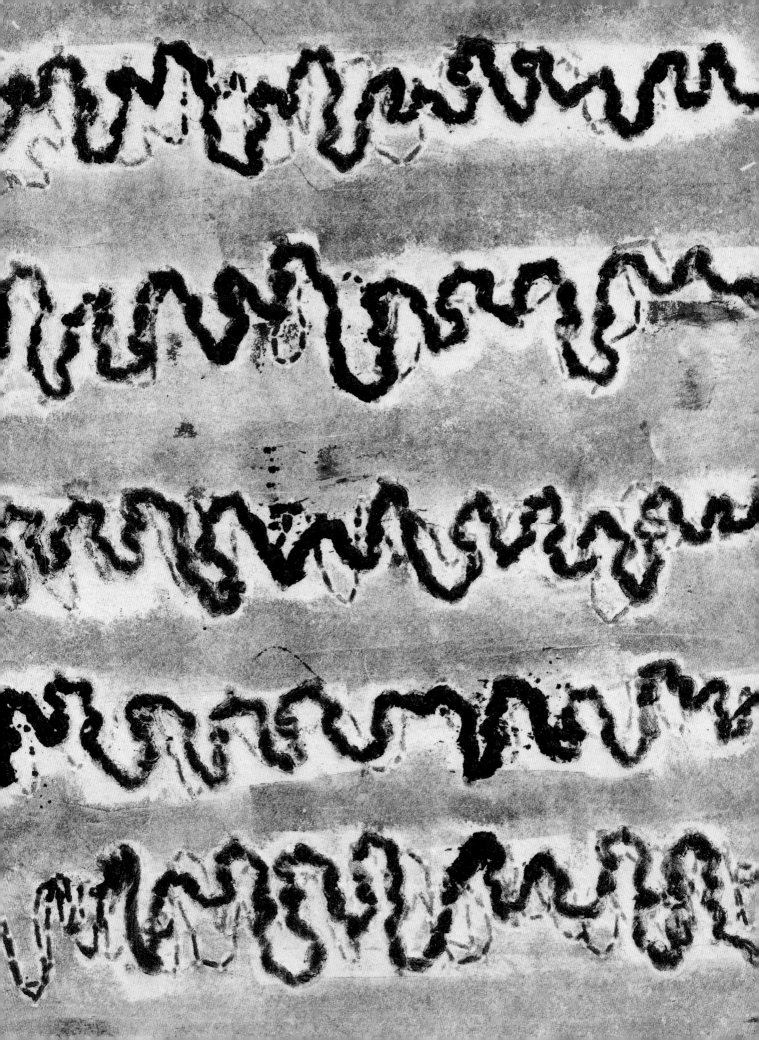

Machine stitching

While not too thick, the ideal collagraphy plate will be stiff, but that doesn't prevent the use of a machine. Although surfaces can be prepared beforehand and then stuck to a plate, embroidery can also be done directly onto various materials to create the plate itself. I find this a very satisfactory method of producing a plate for several reasons: it can be created and ready for use more quickly because no drying time is required for glue; stitching into the surface itself makes holes, giving more presence and immediacy to the stitching itself; and objects can be appliquéd with a machine instead of glue.

Textured fabric pieces that are prepared in advance can be glued to any of the surfaces discussed, although card is the easiest choice. If the stitching is directly into the plate, however, the choice is a little more limited, although it's rather astonishing what a machine will actually stitch through, so do be prepared to try things out.

Needles

I tend to use topstitch needles for most of my embroidery work as these have large eyes in relation to their size and thus protect the threads from breaking. For more difficult surfaces these needles may not be strong enough, in which case jean needles might do the trick. Alternatively, you could use titanium-coated needles, which are also available in a topstitch version. Although these needles can break just as easily as ordinary needles because their inner core is the same, the titanium coating means that they heat up less, which will prevent thread breakage. They also stay sharp longer, which on surfaces such as metal, paper, or card could be a significant help. Needles used for these materials will not be usable for fabrics afterwards, but don't throw them away – put them in a labelled box ready to be reused next time. Plastic can be stitched perfectly well with a topstitch needle, but special needles for plastic/leather exist that ease the passage through plastic if it is a little thick.

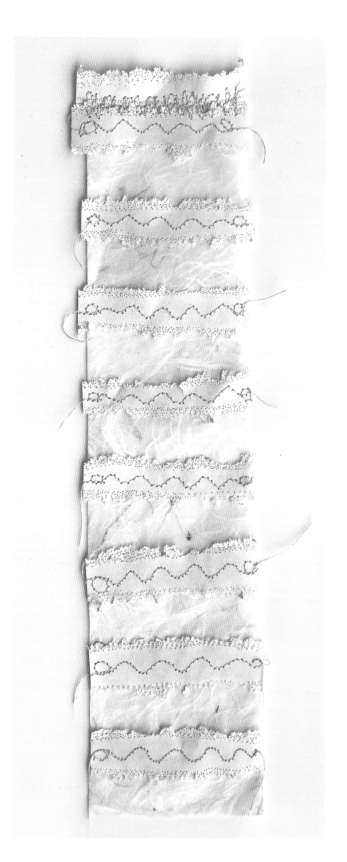

Paper

Paper is easy to stitch into with a machine, but the type you choose will need to be fairly heavyweight, particularly if you are printing by hand. A 300gsm or 450gsm watercolor paper will be stiff enough to make a plate that will last for a few prints. Although it would be difficult to clean afterwards, this won't be a problem in practice because with an inevitably short print run all the prints can be made in one go. To improve the longevity of such a plate it can be glued to another surface and protected accordingly (see Chapter 1).

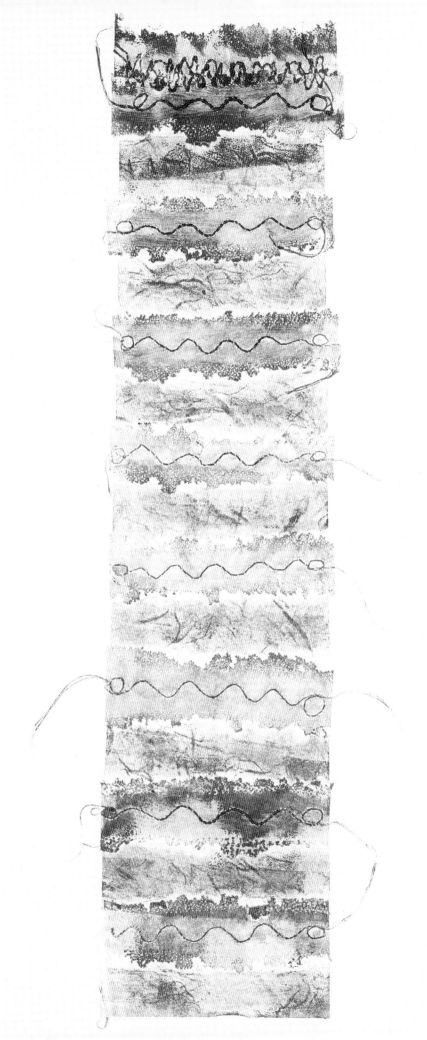

Paper Lace.
The original plate.

Paper Lace. The print was made with the result of an exercise in creating lace effects with paper. A waxy paper was stitched without thread to make holes and to cut through the paper. Strips made in this way were embroidered onto a fine paper with cotton fibers and threads incorporated into it. The result was very delicate, so it was carefully inked with a roller and a brush. Oil-based ink was used, and an etching press.

Card

Any sort of stiff card can be used, although my favorite is matboard. Apart from being relatively easy to stitch into, it is stiff enough to withstand the printing press and will accept some cleaning if properly protected. It also offers a way of recycling the waste cut-outs of the matboard used for framing prints. Whatever card you choose, try stitching through it at first with ordinary stitching – that is, with a normal sewing foot and the feed dog up. Working this way makes it easier to judge the needle and threads to use; if they don't work for ordinary stitching, they will definitely not work for free-motion embroidery. This surface is best stitched at a medium speed: if the work is done too slowly, the machine will have difficulty making the needle go through the cardboard; if too fast, the needle will not pick up quickly enough from the thick surface. Similarly, for free-motion stitching a medium speed with a regular movement is best: if you work too fast, the thickness of the card can mean that it moves on when the needle is still in it.

The card will need to be protected with gesso or varnish or the paper may stick to it when going through the press. This doesn't happen with hand-printing methods, though. The card can be protected before the stitching is added – this doesn't need protection as the paper will not stick to it. Proceeding in this manner also allows the ink to catch on the stitching better, so that it becomes really apparent (see the illustration on page 59).

Metal

Metal shim is available from many embroidery suppliers; a thickness of 0.05mm is fine for stitching into easily. A cheaper option is embossing metal, available from craft suppliers. Cheaper still are tomato purée tubes or even soft-drink cans; beer cans seem to be made of finer metal than soft drink cans and are therefore easier to stitch into. These can all be flattened under a press, with a hammer, or even under the wheels of a car! If there are creases in the metal that is to be used for the plate, they may add to the interest of the print, but avoid them when stitching.

The plate for *Fountain*.

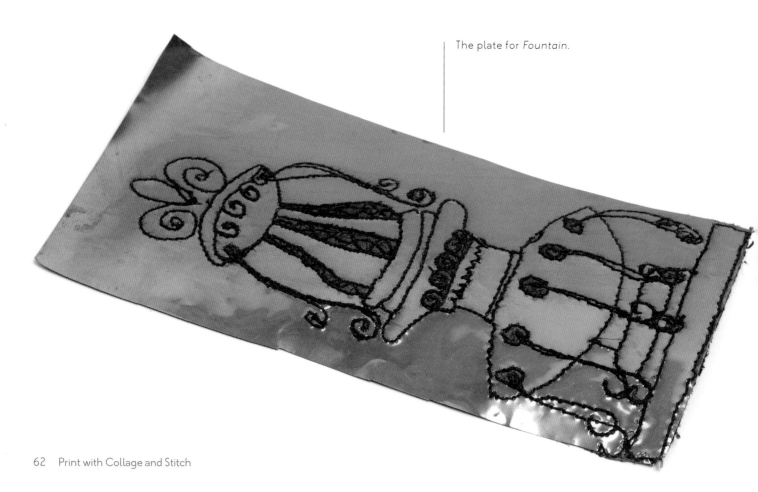

The easiest way to discover the necessary machine speed is by stitching with a foot and the feed dog up: working too fast may cause more thread breakage on this difficult material, but working too slowly can mean that the needle may not pierce the surface. Once this is understood, free-motion embroidery on metal will be easy. It is necessary to place a soft material on the underside of the metal, or the burrs produced on the reverse side through the action of the needle can cause the thread to break. Pellon interfacing, thin felt, or even non-woven soluble fabric are all suitable for this.

The metal doesn't need to be protected with varnish or gesso for printing. It can be wiped clean extremely well, so is a good choice when doing a piece of work where areas of the print are to be kept free of ink. Another advantage of a metal plate is its longevity. The objects attached to it will flatten in time, but they cannot embed themselves into the actual plate as they can with cardboard. This means that a number of print runs can be envisaged, unless the items stitched onto the plate are particularly fragile.

Fountain. A drink can embellished with free-motion stitching was printed on etching paper with an etching press, using oil-based ink. I made the drawing in an Italian town square while eating an ice-cream, which may account for the style of the drawing!

Plastic

Here a stiff but not hard plastic is best, so that the machine needle will go through without too much difficulty. The kind of vinyl or plastic sold to protect books, or used under tablecloths, is ideal, but even a stiff plastic bag will do. Although the plastic may not be completely firm, it will pass through a press without any difficulty, and because of its thinness and malleability it will be a good choice for a collagraph made in a pasta-making machine. Although any machine needle can be used, special needles for leather or PVC, which have dagger-like points rather than round ones, make for easier stitching.

One of the advantages of plastic is that it is very easy to wipe clean and therefore print only the lines or textures added to it. Because of this it is very interesting to use with stitch and embroidery. It also works extremely well with the mixed-color method derived from the Hayter technique that is described in Chapter 5 (see page 89).

Vines in Late Autumn. The stitching caused ripples in the plastic, which have been exploited by the application of ink with a dolly. It was printed on a press with water–washable ink, using the Hayter technique.

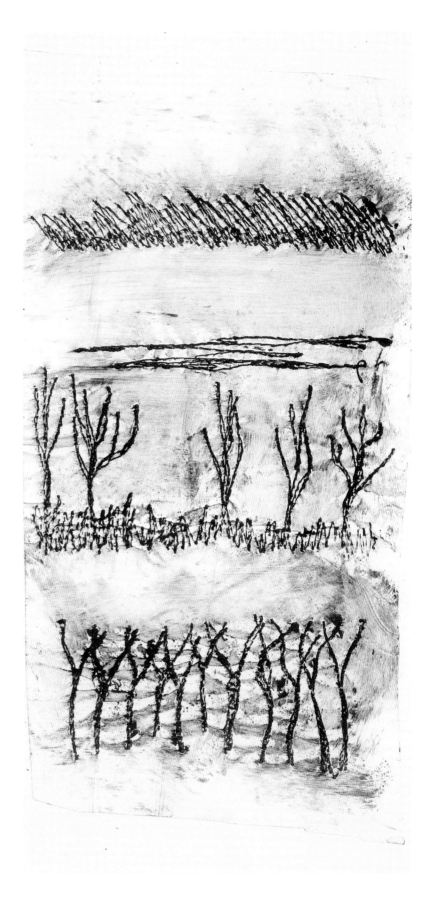

Working without threads

Anyone who has ever stitched on paper, card or metal will probably have already been attracted by the marks that can be made without using any thread in the needle. By experimenting with the set stitches available on the machine, or working with free-motion embroidery, holes can be made in card or metal that will produce an interesting print from either side of the plate. The type of surface created in this way will not make many prints – around three to five seems to be about the limit, although metal will make more than cardboard – but that's no reason not to enjoy these fascinating textures!

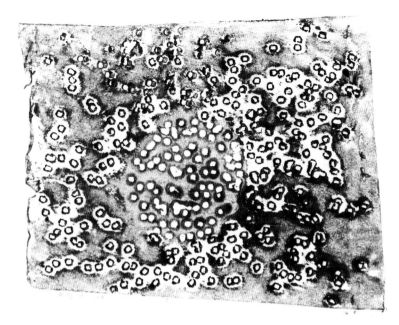

This shows metal with holes punched by a needle without thread. The holes in the circle in the middle were punched from the right side, whereas those in the surrounding area were done from the reverse side. This was worked on a flattened tomato purée tube and printed on an etching press.

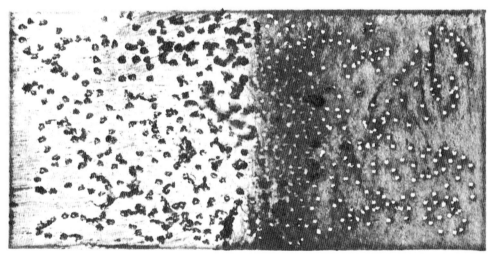

Cardboard with holes punched with a needle without thread from the reverse side (left) and from the right side (right). It was printed on an etching press.

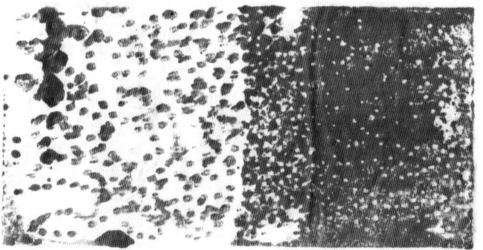

Hand-printed card, using a baren, with holes punched with a needle without thread from the reverse side (left) and from the right side (on the right).

Different stitches and threads

Bear in mind that individual thread color plays a part in the identification of stitching in any embroidery, whereas this will not be the case in a print, where everything is more or less the same color. To help to make sure that the print will be clear, use just one color of thread so that the lines and patterns created can be better exploited.

To get a good result with machine stitching on a collagraphic plate, the thread used is very important. Machine-embroidery threads are likely to be too fine and soft for the job. Topstitch threads or thick quilting threads are useful for fine lines as they are firm and tightly twisted. Use a topstitch needle with a big eye for best results. The texture achieved will be different according to whether the stitching is done on the right side of the work or the reverse side, where the burrs from the passage of the needle will show. On a card plate these burrs will last for only a small number of prints, so it is interesting to print from the reverse side first before continuing from the right side. In order to exploit the reverse side of a metal plate, remember to use non-woven soluble fabric, which can be dissolved before printing, to protect the back of the plate.

For thicker lines, use perle cotton threads or soft embroidery cotton on the bobbin and work from the back of the plate so that the thicker thread appears on the front of it. This is called cable stitch. To do this, loosen the screw on the bobbin case so that the thicker thread can pass through the tension spring; on a horizontal-race machine the spring can simply be bypassed altogether. Set the top tension to a setting of about 6 so that the top thread holds the bobbin thread firmly in place and doesn't get pulled through to the bottom to make big loops. The bobbin thread may form bobbles, in which case, tighten the screw just a little. If the top thread makes loops on the bottom of the work (that is, the right side once finished), tighten the top tension further or release the bobbin screw a little more. Be careful when loosening the bobbin case screw – do this over a tray or embroidery hoop so that the screw doesn't get lost should it spring out.

Working from the reverse side can be difficult on ordinary embroidery, but for a collagraphy plate the drawing can be done simply. This is because, as mentioned earlier, the plate is mirrored once printed, so stitching from the reverse side to a given drawing will actually represent the image as it will be printed. This can also be a useful technique when using writing – from the reverse side of the plate the writing will appear in the right direction, but on the right side it will be reversed so that it will be the correct way round once printed.

A collagraphy plate stitched from the back of the plate, showing the top thread.

This shows the stitching on the bobbin side of the work – the writing, worked in cable stitch with a soft embroidery thread, is in reverse. This is the right side of the plate.

A collagraph printed by hand on calico with thickened dye and a roller.

A collagraph printed with an etching press, using water–washable ink.

When working with appliqué, stitch the applied pieces to the right side of the plate with a normal embroidery thread exactly where you wish the stitching to appear, then follow this line from the reverse side of the plate for the cable stitching.

Any of the decorative stitches on the machine, or just straight lines with the foot and the feed dog up, can be used to create a plate. Alternatively, use free-motion embroidery with a darning foot. Work on the right side of the plate, or on the reverse for the cable stitching.

Handstitching

Handstitching with different thicknesses and textures of thread can provide interesting surfaces for print. If hand printing, the thickness of the threads should not vary too much, and it will be better if the embroidery is kept relatively sparse and clear for the textures to be appreciated. Printing with a press will pick up more detail, so the stitching can be denser and the thread types more varied in thickness, although be careful that the work doesn't become a jumble of textures. As before, it's a good idea to use just one color of thread so that the textures and marks can be better appreciated.

Fabric

One way to create a plate is to hand stitch on fabric first and then glue this to a suitable surface. The chosen fabric could have textural interest too – for example, hessian, silk to retain lots of ink color, or embroidery canvas. Make your choices according to the method of printing to be used. Remember that printing with a press will pick up more detail than hand printing, so textures need to be clearer and more open for hand printing. If you are using thick threads on a fine fabric that is then glued to a plate, threads on the back of the work may show up when printed with a press because of the pressure applied.

Hand–whipped machine–stitched plate, printed on a press with water–washable ink.

Paper

Handstitching can also be done on firm paper and either printed directly or glued to a stiffer surface for printing. In this case the threads on the underside will have less of an impact on the final print.

Card

Pushing a needle through card by hand is not a realistic option, so a number of other possibilities could be considered to facilitate stitching on this surface:

- Make holes in the card first with a punch or other sharp implement, and then use these holes for stitching through.
- Make holes with the largest machine needle you can find – 120/19 is the biggest available. It is then possible, with some force, to pull handstitched threads through these holes.
- Stitch lines onto the card surface with a machine, using straight stitch with a long stitch, and then hand-whip stitch into these stitches.

Hand–whipped machine stitching for a plate.

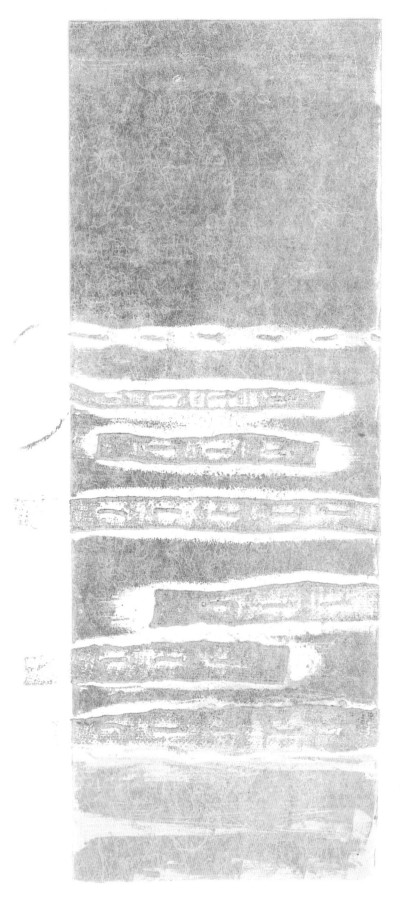

Plastic, Plexiglas and Lucite

Stitching on the type of plastic or vinyl used for protecting tables, books, and so on is very easy by hand. However, this malleable material is very difficult to print by hand with a baren, roller or spoon as it tends to slip around under the paper. If using a baren or spoon, it is easier if the plastic support is attached to a stiffer surface after it has been stitched. The best way of hand printing plastic is with a flower press. For printing with a press it can be used as a flexible plate without any difficulty.

Stitching on Plexiglas or Lucite sounds a little daunting, but, in fact, it is very easy to make holes in this surface with a soldering iron. The best way forwards is to draw the design onto a piece of paper, marking where the holes are needed. Place the drawing underneath a piece of glass, put the Plexiglas (the finer kind will do) on top of the glass, and push the holes through with a hot soldering iron. A mask should be worn for this procedure, and you should work in a well-ventilated area. The burrs made on the back of the Plexiglas can be eliminated with a sharp knife – take care to work away from your body. The burrs could also form a part of the design's texture if it is printed from the back.

An advantage of using hand stitching on Plexiglas is that the threads on the back of the work do not affect the print. They will flatten in time, but this happens fairly slowly as they cannot embed themselves into the Plexiglas.

Pre-punched metal

Stitching through metal by hand is not a realistic option, but there are ways around the problem. See the suggestions given in the section on hand-stitching card on page 67, which apply equally to pre-holed metal.

Seven Waves. Strips of linen fabric stitched to Plexiglas through pre-made holes. This was printed with oil-based ink on an etching press.

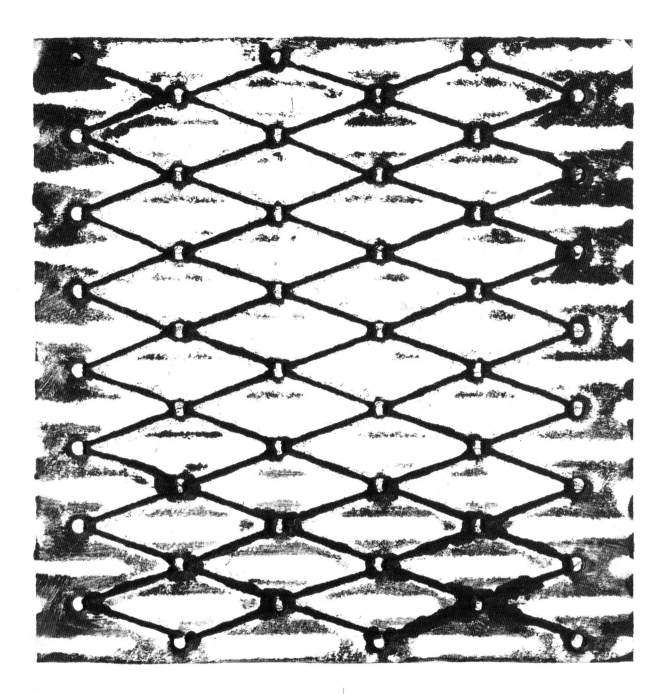

Different stitches and threads

For good results when printing it is best to favor clearly defined individual stitches, such as running stitch, herringbone, fly stitch, or cross stitch, particularly if printing by hand. On a press, which picks up more detail, it is possible to be more experimental with the textures and density of stitching.

Smocking. A pre-punched metal plate from the building industry, which was already slightly sculpted, was stitched with soft embroidery cotton. Inked with water-washable ink, the plate was sandwiched between two smooth metal plates, with several layers of cheap cotton felt placed on top of the paper so as not to ruin expensive etching felts. A car was then used to run over the sandwich of metal plates to make the print (see the illustrations on page 83).

Fabric manipulation and home-made machine lace

Many manipulation techniques using stitch can work well on collagraphy plates. The modified or created textile can be glued to a suitable surface for printing, and it can also be mixed with other media if appropriate. Quilting is one technique that does not work well, as the soft batting would be flattened by the printing process, but the following techniques have all been tried very successfully.

Pin tucks and corded pin tucks

Making pin tucks on the sewing machine is quick and easy with a twin needle. Tighten both top and bottom tensions for best results and, if possible, use a pin-tucking foot. On many machines you can place a cord through the machine plate that will be held by the stitching with the twin needle underneath the work (refer to your machine instruction book for further details). The resulting lines are solid and print well.

Close-up of printed pin tucking.

Urban Landscape. An old jute bag with holes was used as the base for this large plate. Other pieces of fabric were added, including a piece of corded pin tucking, and some textured acrylic paste. It was printed on an etching press with oil-based ink.

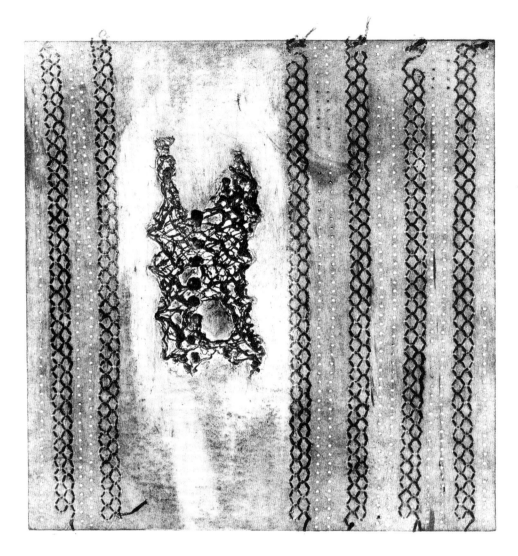

Bodice. The plate was made on card, using some set machine stitches with thread and others without thread to make the holes in the card. The bodice was made on soluble fabric and glued to the plate. French knots were added for the buttons. This was printed with oil-based ink on an etching press.

Pulled work

Pulled work and other openwork or manipulation techniques can be interesting if worked on a large enough scale. This type of fabric manipulation can be done by hand or machine. Again, printing with a press will pick up finer details better, but patience with a baren or a teaspoon will pay off. A flower press may also give reasonable results.

Soluble fabrics

As has already been discussed, lace works extremely well in collagraphy and it can be tempting to create original designs in lace using soluble fabrics. Working with water-soluble fabrics is a good option because when dissolved these leave a residue on the threads used. This residue can be removed from the lace with soaking, but if left on the lace it will be firmer and more stable, and as the

threads are well protected for printing, more prints can be made from the plate. Keep the lace clear, open, and well constructed for a good print.

Working on vanishing muslin, which disappears under a hot iron or heat tool, can also create a range of interesting effects.

An advantage in stitching on dissolvable fabrics, which are then stuck to a suitable printing surface, is that both the needle and the bobbin thread will be present for the print. The stitching to be printed will therefore be thicker than if it had been done directly onto the plate, which would have left only the needle thread present. The disadvantage is that the lines produced may be less distinct, so stitch carefully to a clear design. Satin stitch works well; remember to do this over several lines of straight stitching when working on dissolvable fabric.

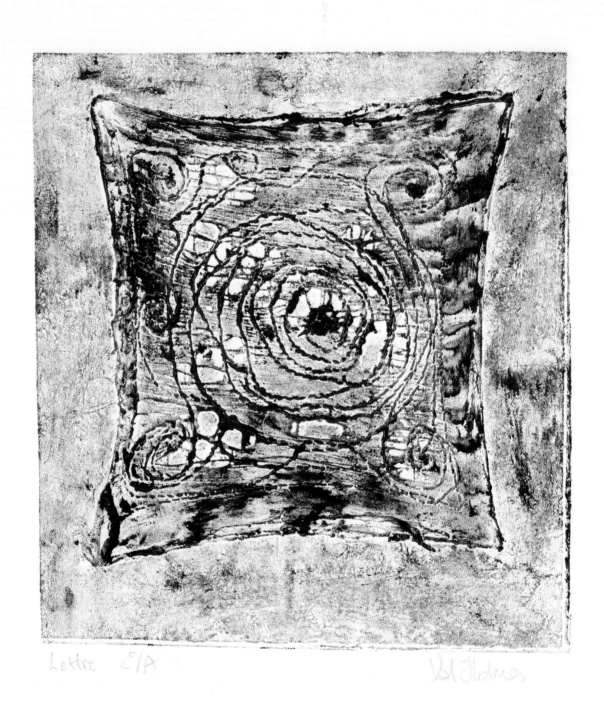

Lettre E/A   Val Holmes

Love Letter. Several layers of polyester organdy were stitched before being pinned to a board and heated with a heat gun to create holes in the structure. The result was then stitched to Lutradur. The plate was printed with oil-based ink on an etching press.

Heat manipulation

Not every surface that looks interesting prints well. Often, items that looked interesting as textiles can look unclear and messy when turned into print. For a print to work there needs to be a fairly clear image – good line, good contrasts. Bear this in mind when creating manipulated surfaces for printing.

Blisters and bumps created when heating Lutradur or Tyvek fabric will tend to flatten when printed, but may, nevertheless, produce interesting textures.

Remember to take the necessary precautions when heating fabrics with a heat tool: wear a mask, work in a well-ventilated area, and keep some water handy in case your fabric or board overheats – although this is unlikely.

There are a few techniques that seem to give good results:

• Lutradur attached to a wooden board before it is heated with a heat tool will make holes rather than blisters. Both the holes and the rough textures around them will print well.

• Strips of burnt Lutradur can also be used. To burn a line into Lutradur, first pin it to a board and then place two wooden planks across it with a gap of ¼" (5 mm) to 1½" (4 cm) between them. Run a heat gun up and down the gully between the planks at a distance of about 2–4" (5–10 cm) until the Lutradur melts. Strips of Lutradur with interesting edges can be made in this way and then attached to a plate. The accuracy of the burnt line and the degree of rough edges will depend on the distance left between the planks.

• Working with Lutradur, or several layers of polyester organdy, you can stitch simple shapes that will form a lace structure. This must be done with a natural-fiber thread in the needle and bobbin of the machine, otherwise the thread will melt. Rayon, cotton, and silk threads are all suitable. Fix the fabric to a board with drawing pins for heating with a heat tool. Melt the fabric with this (see the instructions above) as much as desired back to the stitching lines. Glue the result to a suitable surface to make the plate. Lutradur is best protected with a varnish or gesso so that the paper does not stick to it during printing.

• The texture of Lutradur itself, without any heating, is also interesting, and will print very well with both a baren and a press.

• The surface of polyester organdy inks up in a very satisfactory way.

Experimenting with brodagraphy

Remember that there are almost as many ways of creating and interpreting collagraphy plates as there are makers, so experiment with the stitches and fabric manipulation techniques that you enjoy best and see how they print. If you don't like the result, you might find that it could be improved with stitching later. Keep notes of what you do to produce the different prints that you create, so that you can reproduce success and reduce

disappointment. Remember, though, that nothing is really a failure; it's just part of the learning process.

Collagraphy printing is not a precise art, and it is the surprises that can keep up your interest and desire for experimentation. For this reason, I find it better to judge a set of prints the day after I have made them as then I can judge them for what they actually are, and not what I expected them to be.

CHAPTER ‹ 4 ›

PRINTING WITHOUT A PRESS

Other printing options

Using an etching press is the most satisfactory method for exploiting intaglio and relief printing. It is much easier to deal with objects of differing heights on a plate when using a press than with any other method. However, not having access to an etching press doesn't mean that you can't enjoy collagraph printing, as there are quite a few other means worth trying and these can give quite satisfactory results too.

The first group is really about those hand-printing methods traditionally used for relief printing such as lino printing and woodblock printing. The second group looks at ways of developing simple hand-printing presses on which, with enough pressure, the plate may be printed in relief and intaglio.

Basic utensils for hand printing include a roller or rolling pin, spoon and baren. Here two types of baren are shown: a student version of a traditional *hon* baren covered with a bamboo leaf, and a wood baren with felt protection. A toothbrush can also be useful, and of course you can use your fingers. Use a roller, sponge brushes or brushes for inking up.

Hand-printing methods for collagraphy

In general, more ink or other medium is required on the plate when hand printing than when using a traditional etching press. For this reason, choose water-based media as oil-based ink can look unsightly if sticky, heavy patches are accidentally left when printing. A sponge roller or sponge brushes will leave more of the medium on the plate than an ordinary paintbrush or rubber roller.

Using a roller or rolling pin

Rollers of different dimensions can be purchased at various prices, but a heavy marble pastry roller or a silicone one will also do the trick. To get a good result when using a roller the plate will have to be very even, with no great difference in the heights of the objects glued or stitched onto its surface. The print will be printed very simply in relief – that is, from the raised surfaces of the objects on the plate – and the best results will be obtained if this is taken into consideration and exploited. Lace, textured pastes, and other highly textured surfaces don't show up very well with this method, but simple stitched lines can be useful, and particularly thin card cut out to make the required shapes and patterns.

For this method I have found that it is best to have a fair amount of color present, so use acrylic paint, acrylic ink, or the thickened dye mix described on page 44, and apply the medium with a sponge roller or sponge brush so that it is evenly distributed.

Place the plate face upwards on a table at a height that is comfortable for pressing heavily with a roller, put a piece of paper (fine papers work better) onto the plate, and then roll with pressure. Be very careful not to move the paper around. This is less likely to occur if you roll from the middle of the print towards the edge. Repeat this action until the print is satisfactory – lift up a corner of the paper from time to time to check the result.

Experience will show how much wet medium is required in relation to the pressure applied. Too much ink and too much pressure will spoil the image with smudged lines; too little ink and pressure will result in an unclear image. Although this method does work on paper prints, I find it better for printing on fabric, which is less likely to move around. Printing methods using barens of various types seem more suitable for printing on paper.

Using a teaspoon

A teaspoon is an extremely good tool for collagraph printing. This is the homespun version of the traditional printing baren, most frequently used for woodblock printing. Start by inking up the plate with a sponge roller, in order to apply enough wet medium. Then place a fine piece of paper over the plate. The best types for this process are the fine Japanese-style papers suitable for woodblock printing. These are strong and malleable, while thin enough to be worked into the print's more difficult areas. For greater malleability the paper can be placed beforehand in a tray of water, blotted and allowed to dry until it is just damp. Note that the optimum time spent in the water differs between papers, so be careful that your paper doesn't become so soggy that it falls to pieces. In general, just dipping these fine papers in the water and taking them out immediately will be enough.

Now, with the back of the spoon, rub the paper all over to make the print. The curves of the spoon enable you to achieve greater detail from the more textured areas than is possible when using a roller. Don't use the very edges of the spoon, though, or the paper might tear. For larger, flatter areas, use a wooden or bamboo spoon. If the paper shows signs of breaking up, put some tissue paper over it to protect it and then continue working. Once the paper has been thoroughly worked over with the spoon, try rubbing the more difficult textural areas with the ends of your fingers. This can really improve the results.

This method allows a wider choice of media to be used to create the plate than the roller method, as different thicknesses can be dealt with, to a certain extent, by using the spoon with dexterity. Because the level of pressure can be varied in different areas of the plate, more delicate materials can also be used in its construction. Some organic materials that won't withstand a press may be used successfully when printing with a spoon if enough care is taken. Textured acrylic pastes and carborundum can also work to an extent, and with patience and care some laces and stitching will print with this method.

Autumn in the Languedoc. Printed with a roller using thickened dyes on calico.

Trees on the Loire.
The plate was made with textured acrylic paste and lace, two very difficult materials for hand printing, but by using a spoon and fingers, a print was possible. Acrylic lino-print ink was used on 40gsm Japanese paper.

Using a baren

The *hon* baren is the traditional Japanese tool for woodblock printing. There are many and varied versions, according to the type of carving and design used for the woodblock print. The body consists of a disk of very finely made cardboard, although wood ones are also available, with a flat coil of twisted bamboo on one side, covered with a bamboo leaf that is twisted to form a handle. Lesser-quality *hon* barens, made with synthetic or paper coils, can be purchased online, as can a version made with bamboo leaf-covered ball bearings. All of these real *hon* barens are so expensive that it would be more economical to invest in a press!

The cheapest student-quality baren is cardboard covered with a bamboo leaf. This can wear out quite quickly on rough surfaces, but otherwise is quite easy to use. The flat surface is good for relief printing and the edges can be used for areas with more detail and texture. You may find it useful to use a combination of this type of implement for some areas of a print, and a spoon or fingers for others.

The bamboo leaf on a real *hon* baren should be oiled from time to time, or left on an oiled cloth during printing. Camellia oil is traditionally recommended for this, or good-quality flower or plant oil. If heavily used on many different surfaces, the bamboo leaf on the baren will not have a particularly long life, and although the baren can be re-covered if you have a decent supply of bamboo leaves, this is probably best left to the professionals. The student-quality baren does not merit this kind of treatment, as its lifespan will be pretty short anyway and its cost makes it a replaceable item.

Other types of baren also exist, with a wooden handle that fits into the palm of the hand and a soft pad at the other end, or with a wooden handle and a silicone roller. The latter is not especially useful for most collagraph printing unless the plate is particularly flat. I have found the version with the wooden handle and the soft pad useful for spreading out the paper or fabric to be printed onto the printing plate. Using this tool helps the paper to stick well to the surface, and you can continue with the burnishing afterwards using either the tool or a spoon. It also works well when using thickened dye as the chosen medium, but otherwise the firmness of the bamboo baren is more useful.

Work with a baren in the same way as a spoon, trying to use the tackiness of the ink on a large flat surface of the plate to hold down the paper when you first start. Work out from this area, using smooth, curved motions. Continue working in this way with varying amounts of pressure, according to the profile and quality of the plate. Small circular rubbing motions will help to get the most out of the more difficult areas of the plate.

If the paper shows signs of wear, there are several options you can consider:

- Make sure that all the rubbing is done along the grain of the paper and not against it or at an angle.
- Make sure that the paper has not been left in the water for too long – it may be that too much of the size has been removed.
- Protect the paper before continuing to rub with the baren. There are special papers for this, but tissue paper can also be used.
- Any distressing could be allowed to happen and become part of the work. This could be embroidered into or applied to another paper or textile later.

Other similar methods

All sorts of ways of transferring the ink from plate to paper can be improvised. Your fingers can get into the crevices of a very textured plate better than any implement. Rubbing the paper onto the plate with fingers, having first placed it in position with a baren, can be very satisfying, and because fingers are softer they are less likely to wear out the paper. A toothbrush can also be used for this. A damp toothbrush will pick up more ink from the plate if your medium is water-based, although care must be taken not to smudge the image too much. This can, however, produce a soft watercolor result.

Wood. Acrylic ink was used with the intention of attempting an intaglio and relief print with this difficult plate. This was possible for the etching press print on page 24, but due to the closeness of the threads it proved impossible using a baren and fingers. The Japanese paper was therefore put onto the plate and pushed into it with a damp toothbrush to pick up the acrylic ink. It had to be not too wet or the ink would bleed. This technique also works with oil-based ink, as the water will not cause it to bleed.

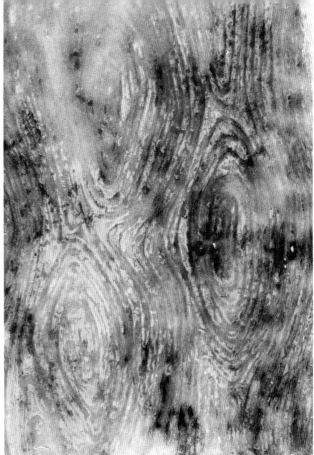

Autumn in the Languedoc. Using the same plate as for *Autumn in the Languedoc* on page 77, this print was made on 18gsm Japanese paper with a bamboo-leaf baren.

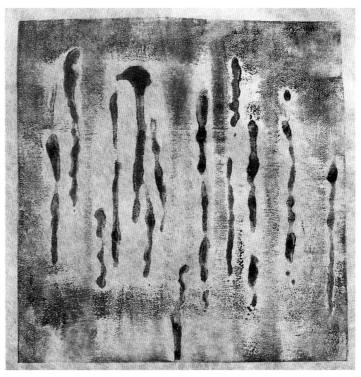

Refugees. This was printed on 18gsm Japanese paper with a baren. The paper wore through in places and a red fabric was placed behind.

Simple press techniques

Although the techniques below refer to preparing the plate by inking up with a roller, once you start using press techniques, and therefore more pressure on the plate, you will be able to experiment more with the inking, working into the depths of the plate and the relief. These techniques are developed further in Chapter 5.

A flower press

If you don't own a tailor-made flower press, it is very easy and cheap to make a simple version of one that will work well for collagraphs. Instructions for how to do this are given on page 122.

To make a print with a flower press:

1. Place the inked plate for printing onto the wood base. Less ink is required for a print made in this kind of press than with the other hand-printing methods, but more ink is required than with a traditional etching press. Ink can be applied with an ordinary paintbrush or rubber roller, or with a sponge roller or brush, but apply slightly less medium than when hand printing without any kind of press.
2. Place a dampened piece of paper (soaked and then dried a little as usual) on top of the plate. Finer papers work best.
3. Put several – two to four – pieces of felt or blanket on top of this. The number required will depend on the thickness of the felt or blanket, and also on the thickness and unevenness of the plate. If the plate is very uneven, it will be worth using more padding.
4. Place the second piece of wood over the sandwich, aligning the holes with the screws on the base. Position the washers and screw the wing nuts down as hard as possible. The washers will take the pressure off the wood immediately around the screws and the wing nuts.
5. Weights can also be placed on top of the wood, as evenly as possible; you will find that the wing nuts can be screwed down more under this additional weight.

1. A flower press set up with a print and the paper in place.

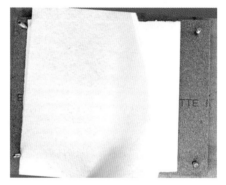

2. The felts are put on top.

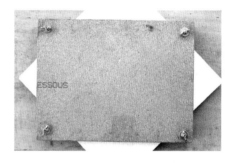

3. The top piece of wood is screwed down.

4. The top piece of wood is taken off, showing the print and the plate.

6. To remove the print, unscrew the wing nuts and undo the press, then peel the paper off the plate carefully.

Adjustments in the amount of ink applied to the plate and the number of felts or blankets used may be necessary in order to get a good result.

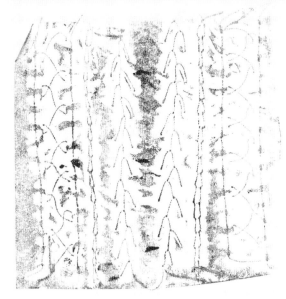

Handstitching on a plastic plate, printed with water-washable etching ink on 300gsm etching paper with a flower press.

As above but with a screw-down hand press. This simple press provides more pressure for the print than a flower press.

1. A screw-down hand press with the plate, paper and felts in place.

2. The press is screwed down as tightly as possible.

3. The press is released and the felts lifted to reveal the back of the print.

Other types of hand press

Other types of hand press exist, with either a screw system to exert pressure or with a lever to produce pressure by hand or with the user's weight. These are used for woodblock and lino printing, for pressing home-made paper, or for book-making. It is sometimes possible to find these in the second-hand marketplace, and it is not too complicated to make this type of press. More information is given in Chapter 9.

Although these presses do not exert as much pressure as a traditional etching press, which is designed to push the paper into the smallest or deepest of crevices in a metal plate to find the ink, they will nevertheless apply more pressure than all the others so far discussed and can therefore be a useful alternative to an etching press.

Because more pressure is applied, less ink is required than for the previous hand-printing techniques, and oil-based ink or water-washable etching ink can be used easily. The paper chosen can also be thicker than for the previous methods.

To use this kind of press:

1. Place the plate on the base of the press and then cover with paper, dampened as usual.
2. Put a couple of soft felts or blankets on top, the number required depending on the amount of relief on the plate.
3. Screw down the press, or use the lever, with as much force or weight as possible.
4. To see the resulting print, unscrew the press, or lift the lever, and pull back the felts or blankets carefully. If it is not clear enough, add or remove a felt or blanket layer, according to the complexity of the plate – experiment to obtain a good result.

A pasta-making machine

You will need a pasta-making machine of good quality to take the pressure required for printing. The base plate of the machine may get in the way when you put a collagraphy plate through, so if necessary, take this off and try to come up with a new way of clamping the machine to the table. Once all this has been achieved, there are a few more useful rules in order to obtain a good print:

• Use a flexible plate – cardboard, paper, or malleable plastic will be easiest and will help to avoid altering the pasta-making machine too much.
• Keep the surface of the plate as even as possible. If it is too thick, or has too much relief, there will be problems getting it through the machine or getting a good print.
• As with a flower press, more pressure is applied, so a little less ink is required on the plate. Experiment to achieve a good result.
• Use water-based ink, dyes, or acrylics to make for easier cleaning of the press afterwards. Clean it immediately after use, using lots of soapy water, and you may even be able to use it for making pasta! Do make sure, however, that it is scrupulously clean if you are going to reuse it for this purpose.

Bearing in mind the inherent difficulties of using a pasta-making machine for printing and the fact that it really achieves only a relief print, a flower press seems a more reasonable alternative.

A mangle

It is possible to create something similar to a printing press, that will exert quite a substantial amount of pressure, out of an old mangle. Unfortunately, though, mangles are becoming rare, so this is only a solution for the lucky people who are able to find one. If you do not already possess one, however, be careful about over-investing in a purchase – a cheap press may cost less. Mangles vary, so even if you do find one, you will then have to imagine how to adapt it to become the press of your dreams! There are a few blogs and websites available where people who have managed the conversion give advice; some have even successfully used mangles for printing etchings. As collagraphs are generally less demanding than etchings in terms of the pressure needed, this suggests that a mangle would be an excellent solution for a press.

A garden roller

To use a garden roller as a press, place the plate, dampened paper and a felt or two onto a very flat surface, then run the roller over it carefully so as not to move the paper. Make sure that the roller is scrupulously clean beforehand or it will transfer imprints from gravel or similar to the print. Once it has been cleaned, put a blanket down before doing the work so that the roller is kept on a very clean surface.

A car

You can even use a car as a press! Place the plate, dampened paper and a felt or two onto a very flat surface or a piece of metal. Put a second piece of sturdy metal on top to prevent the imprint of the car tire marking the print and then run the car over it. Get someone's help in lining up the wheel of the car on the metal beforehand. Even plaster prints can withstand this method of printing, the only drawback being that the width of the plate is limited to the width of the car's tire.

A roadroller or steamroller

I've seen one of these at an etching festival, where it was used to make an enormous print. Of course, it's not the sort of thing we all keep in the garage…

A car as a press

1. The inked plate is placed on a piece of metal in front of the car wheel.

2. Dampened paper is placed on top of the plate.

3. Felts are put in position.

4. Another piece of metal is placed on top of the felts.

5. The car is rolled over the plate.

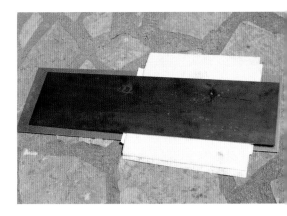

6. The sandwich once the car has driven over it. The final print can be seen on page 69.

CHAPTER ‹ 5 ›

PRINTING WITH A PRESS

The etching press

The most effective way of printing collagraphy plates is with an etching press. Constructed with a very heavy roller and a screw system to provide even more pressure if required, it is designed to push the paper into the fine incised lines of etched metal to produce an intaglio print. This type of press is capable of printing both the relief areas and the crevices of any plate with ease. See chapter 9 for more information.

We have already seen how different types of rollers and brushes, particularly sponge brushes, are used to ink the plate for hand-printing methods. When printing with an etching press, very little ink is required, and it can be applied not only with a rubber roller but also with brushes and rags. Plates can also be wiped using tarlatan (stiff cotton muslin) to create nuances in the colors and

ink density. With an etching press textures and depths in the plate can be more extreme, and printing in intaglio and relief more easily achieved. The resulting prints will become richer in texture, nuance, and color. The different methods of ink application, which can be combined to include color mixing and layering on the plate itself, offer a large and fascinating area of exploration and discovery.

Details of Venice. The leftover ink on the glass plate after etching included gold and it seemed a shame to waste it, so I made a print onto paper. Gold transfer foil was added to the paper, and then finally this collagraph print was printed with an etching press onto the prepared paper.

Working with a roller

The ink, whichever type is used, needs to be put on the plate quite sparingly, as the pressure from the press will enable the paper to reclaim most of the available ink. If too much ink has been applied, the result will be unclear, with patches of ugly encrusted ink.

The following exercise explains how to create a print on an etching press. Inked with a roller, it will show the relief of the plate in a single color, which is a useful way of indicating where to put other colors subsequently, and how to use the depths and profiles of the plate. For the purposes here, use a primary color to start off with. Once you have completed this step, the next one will be to see what happens if the depths of the textures – that is, the intaglio elements – of the plate are printed too.

You will need:
• A roller or two – 4" (10cm) and 2" (5cm) are useful sizes
• A small artist's palette knife
• The ink of your choice – oil-based ink or water-washable etching ink are the best for printing with a press, but try whatever is available.
• A large piece of glass with the edges either polished or protected with masking tape. The size doesn't really matter, but 15¾" × 19½" (40 × 50cm) should be the absolute minimum. A very large piece of glass is better as it allows for the colors to be developed and mixed over a session of work. A marble slab could also be used.
• An extender. For water-washable etching ink there is a special oil extender, which will be available from the same manufacturer as the ink, to liquefy the ink a little if necessary. For oil-based ink linseed oil can be used, but I prefer the easy-wipe extender available from some etching suppliers. This is used when the ink seems too stiff to be applied in the desired way, which may occur when using a roller and is very likely to occur when using a brush or dolly for intaglio printing. Just add a small amount to the ink and work in with a small artist's palette knife.

For the follow-up experiments you will need:
• Some old paintbrushes, the stiff type used for acrylic or oil painting
• About 3¼' (1m) tarlatan (stiff cotton muslin).

Method:
1. Squeeze a knob of ink onto the inking slab.
2. Using the roller, roll into a little of the ink and roll it out onto the slab until it is very flat. This will make a slight splashing noise and the ink will form small peaks on the slab because at this stage there is still too much ink on the roller. Spread the ink out further until it no longer feels sticky and the splashing noise disappears.
3. Now roll over the plate to be printed. Take care as you do this because any imperfection in the application of the ink, such as marks crossing or variations in intensity, will show when the plate is printed.
4. If the plate is highly textured, roll on the ink in different directions, and use a small roller. For extreme textures it may be necessary to use a brush or dolly, but more of that later (see pages 88–90).
5. Any area of the plate that looks too shiny and as if it has too much ink on it can be carefully wiped with a piece of tarlatan. If the whole plate looks far too inked, it can be run through the press on a piece of craft paper first, instead of ruining an expensive piece of etching or watercolor paper. I have found this a very useful technique as it takes off just enough ink to ensure that the next print on the quality paper will be good without having to re-ink the plate. Another advantage is that because the craft paper is used dry and therefore takes less ink, the result can be quite acceptable and may therefore be usable, either as it is or embroidered, afterwards. If the etching paper had been used, however, the ink would have bled or been left in unsightly patches.
6. Put the inked plate face upwards on the bed of the press. Carefully place a prepared piece of damp paper on top of the plate – do not move the paper once it is in position as there may already be some ink on it.

7. Place two or three pieces of felt on top of the paper. Special thick, firm felt for etching presses and printing is available from specialist suppliers. It is essential to use felts for this process: the bed of the press and the roller are metal, and the felts provide the necessary flexibility in order for the paper to mould around the plate. If you are using someone else's printing press, it may be a good idea to buy your own felts as they can be damaged in use. For example, inks can seep through thinner papers or fabric and print onto the felts, and some hard materials on the plate, such as buttons or metal, can actually pierce the paper and even the felts. Be aware of this and take the necessary precautions, either by buying your own felts or by using old blankets under a precious piece of felt. To engage the felts under the roller of the press, the top felt should overlap the other felts just a little on the leading edge, so that the roller takes up the single thickness first and more easily.

8. Roll the print through the press. You will feel the force of the press and the additional force as the roller makes contact with the plate. It is important to keep up a slow, even speed and not stop during this process. Pressure can be added to the roller by screwing down the pressure at the side of the press, or by adding more felts; but for this first print, do not use any additional pressure on the press – just try with the weight of the roller to see how it goes. Lift a corner of the paper to look at the result and if it is not good enough, the press can be rolled backwards over the plate, perhaps with a little more pressure if necessary.

9. Carefully take off the felts and the paper to see the print.

Reflections of Venice. This first print from the plate used for the print on page 25 was made by applying Indian Yellow oil–based ink to the plate with two sizes of roller. The first print gives an indication of how it can be improved by adding other colors in the depths of the plate, and perhaps other colors in relief as well.

Working with a paintbrush

Inks can be applied in quite a precise way with a brush, and brush marks may even be left on the surface of the plate to create more interest.

To work with a paintbrush, proceed as follows:

1. Use the same color as before, well rolled out on the glass surface.
2. Take the ink onto a stiff brush. It is important that the brush is almost dry as it pushes the ink into the depths of the plate, to avoid chunks of wet ink. Work the ink all over the plate, into the deep crevices and the nooks and crannies. Use tarlatan where necessary to wipe off areas with too much ink present. Nuances can also be created by the careful rubbing off of colors.
3. Now choose a second color – perhaps another primary color, which would create a secondary color if mixed with the first ink. Roll out as before and then roll this onto the relief of the plate. Use tarlatan as above if necessary.
4. Print through the press as before, onto a new piece of paper, taking the same precautions and care.

Compare the results of the first print made with just one color in relief with the second print made with two colors in relief and intaglio. In the second print, where the relief area was inked with a roller, and perhaps in some areas with a brush as well, a third color will appear as the inks mix to form a secondary color.

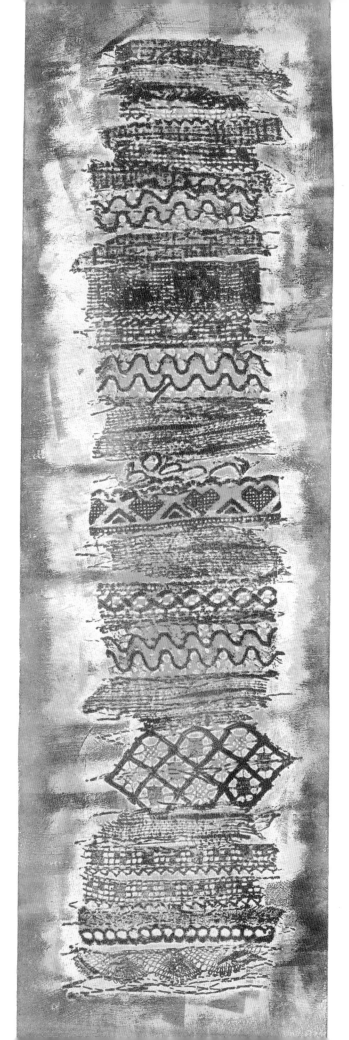

Reflections of Venice. Indian Yellow was brushed into the depths of the plate after the first relief print and Burnt Sienna was rolled onto the relief of the plate before being reprinted. See also page 25 for a multicolored version.

Venice. The plate was made by machine stitching onto plastic with a sewing thread. Here the thread was simply given a coating of black ink, which was carefully cleaned off the plastic around the stitching with tarlatan and kitchen towel. Water–washable ink was used.

Venice. Blue, yellow and red inks were separately wiped over the plate with a tarlatan rag; each time a little of the ink was allowed to remain on some areas of the plate. The stitching retained the ink even when it was wiped off the surrounding areas. Water–washable ink was used.

Reprinting the image with the third primary color in some areas of the plate will result in a print containing all three primaries, all three secondary colors and even black where all three primary colors mix. This technique of simultaneous color printing is borrowed from the British painter and printmaker Stanley William Hayter (1901–88) who, by working with different levels of viscosity in the inks that he used and rollers of different densities, perfected a method of printing etchings with the three primary colors in a single operation. Using his method, the ink in the crevices of the etchings becomes black where the three colors mix, and the three primaries are left on the surface of the plate, or rubbed off in different areas, to allow for them to show, and for the three secondary colors to develop with different nuances and densities of color, as desired by the artist.

I have worked on a collagraphy version of this technique using either cardboard, metal or plastic. In the case of cardboard, this is first protected with acrylic varnish or medium and the card is then stitched into; no further protection or varnish is added. In the case of metal or plastic, these are stitched onto and used without any protection.

Apply each primary color in turn to the plate, using a brush or dolly (see page 90) and making sure that the ink is worked well into the stitching from all directions. After the application of each color any undesirable excess ink can be wiped off the plate, leaving it only in those areas where it is required. The plate can now be printed in the normal way. The stitched areas should be almost black and the other colors will be present as desired.

Working with a dolly

A dolly is a ball of tarlatan wrapped in a piece of tarlatan, using either one or two pieces of cloth to create a tool that resembles a small doll's head. It can be used to apply small areas of color to different parts of the plate. A dolly enables you to rub the ink well into the nooks and crannies of the plate and into the different textures.

To use this tool, roll out the ink well before taking it onto the dolly so that there aren't patches of very wet ink on the dolly. Working with a dolly allows precision in the quantities of ink placed on the plate, which can be rubbed out to create nuances and depth of color, particularly when the plate has been sealed with a smooth varnish or medium, rather than gesso.

A dolly loaded with black ink.

1. Red ink on a large dolly ready for rubbing onto the plate. Note that the plate had been printed before, which is why there is already apparent color on it.

2. Rubbing the color onto the plate.

3. Yellow is taken up onto another dolly.

4. Yellow is rubbed onto the plate.

5. Blue is taken up onto a new dolly.

6. Blue is rubbed onto the plate.

7. The plate is placed onto the bed of the press.

8. Paper is placed over the plate.

9. The felts are put into position.

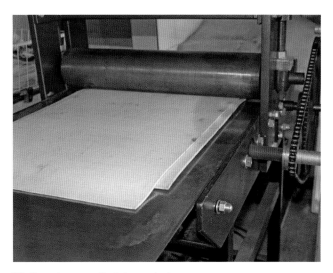

10. The plate is rolled through the press.

11. The felts are lifted to show the printed paper; the texture on the paper indicates that the pressure was strong enough.

12. The paper is lifted to reveal the print.

Fossil I. The original plate was made with plaster on cardboard. It was printed on etching paper with oil–based ink on an etching press.

Wiping the plate

The art of etching is very much to do with the way in which the plate is wiped after inking. Although collagraphy is very different, nevertheless a print can be improved if the plate is wiped to allow for the different degrees of ink take-up according to the textures of the plate. To do this, make a dolly as before, but with up to 1 yd (91.5 cm) of tarlatan. The ball of cloth and its tarlatan cover should be quite big in the palm of your hand so that it is possible to remove ink from certain areas of the plate. By wiping in one direction and changing the strength of the color, a greater illusion of depth in the design can be created.

Adding colors

It is possible to build up interesting prints by adding color either to the depth of the plate or to the relief elements. For example, areas of the plate can be brushed with specific colors to add meaning to the print. To exploit the complexity of color in this way I print off all the prints at once, not cleaning the plate between each printing, so that the colors can mix and affect each other. If the prints start to get too heavy, or a mark is made that doesn't work, the plate can be wiped with a ball of tarlatan before continuing. Some of the ink will remain to affect future colors, but not too much. If necessary, a plate can be cleaned between prints. Start by printing off the plate onto craft paper to reduce the amount of ink present, and then clean off the ink using water, vegetable oil, or the appropriate solvent, depending on the ink chosen.

To work successfully with this method of gradually building up colors for simultaneous color printing, it is best to look at the last print that was made from the plate, rather than the plate itself, to get an idea of where color needs to be added for the next print. The uncleaned plate will be covered in color, and it is very easy to be fooled into thinking that all those colors are still available on the plate for printing, whereas the color densities on the previous print will provide a more accurate guide.

Although I have suggested using primary colors as a starting point for experimenting in the way that Hayter did, this technique can also work with different colors chosen for the plate according to the subject matter and the specific colors desired. So mix your colors as required, but try to consider how they will cross over and what mixes are likely to happen as a result.

When the color build-up on the prints starts to be really satisfactory it's a good time to make a few prints onto some prepared fabric, so that they can be used for textile embroideries.

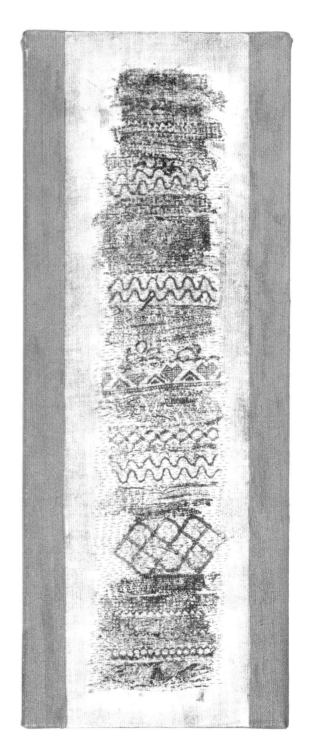

Venice. The same plate was used as on page 87, printed on linen sheeting. This was then painted down the sides with gold bronzing powders mixed with acrylic wax and handstitched with a running stitch in fine gold thread.

Printing in black

When I feel that I have fully experimented with the colors that can be added to my plate, or I feel that the plate is nearing the end of its life, I make a print in black, first with a roller, and then wiping back with a dolly for a second print. The colors that may already be present on the plate will be faintly visible through the black, adding a depth to the print. It is this print that will most resemble a traditional etching in the print run.

As a plate reaches the end of its life the pressure on the roller may have to be increased in order to continue getting good prints. At a certain point you will notice that the plate has flattened so much that the details are becoming unclear. You will be the best judge of when this loss of detail is no longer acceptable in relation to the initial idea.

Preparing the paper

For best results it is worth soaking the paper before printing as this makes the fibers more supple. This means that the paper will more easily enter the crevices of the plate and will be less likely to crease or tear. Soak the paper in a tray for about fifteen minutes prior to printing and hang it up to dry. When barely, but evenly, damp, the paper can be used for printing. For ease of use I prepare a quantity of paper for a printing session by leaving it to soak in a deep tray normally used for paper-making, but a cat litter tray may be a good option. The sheets of paper are then hung with pegs to dry on an old clotheshorse. Once they have reached the correct degree of dampness – that is, they feel damp to the touch but not wet – I put them in a plastic bag ready for use. The paper can be kept in the bag for several days ready for printing. If it is not all used, allow it to dry – it can be soaked again for another session and will be fine as long as this process is not repeated too often. Note that the paper used for the new water-washable etching ink needs to be a little less damp than with oil-based ink.

Refugees. The last print was printed in black, but the previous blue ink was still very present.

River Bank. After nine other prints in color, this last one was made in black, rubbed on with a dolly. Blue ink is still visible. The plate was made with acrylic paste and bits of fabric on a card base, and it was printed with oil–based ink on an etching press.

Variations in printing from one plate

As we have seen in Chapter 2, there are many different paper or textile surfaces that can be used for printing on, and many ways of altering them before printing.

The advantage of printing with an etching press is that the additional pressure it produces enables all sorts of different surfaces to be used, as the thickness of the paper or textile chosen will be pressed into the textures of the plate. So be adventurous and try altering papers using techniques such as *chine-collé*, for example. To bring life to a textile print, textiles can be dyed, patched,

stitched on, or appliquéd before being used. They can be printed on with oil-based ink or water-washable etching ink; oil-based ink will not wash out and water-washable ink will be fast once dry. There will be a change in the feel of the fabric surface, but this will be slight if the ink is used sparingly, as suggested.

When printing fabrics the ink can penetrate the material and go through to the felts. To prevent this, try putting a piece of craft paper or old fabric between the fabric to be printed and the felts to absorb any excess ink.

Broken Blinds.
Thickened dyes were
used on a plate made
from an old bamboo
place mat. Printing in
intaglio and relief with
wet media is more
difficult than with
finely layered inks,
but using blue on the
relief and yellow in
the crevices, which
mixed to create green
here and there, made
the view through the
blinds more
interesting. This was
printed on calico on
an etching press.

Intaglio dye printing

When printing with dyes or fabric paints it is necessary to use a little more medium on the plate, so apply it with a sponge roller or, better still, a sponge paintbrush. The dye or fabric paint requirements vary according to the type of fabric to be printed, so practise using these media to find out how much paint or dye to apply. This can be done by applying varying amounts of each medium to different bands of the plate with a sponge paintbrush and then putting this through the press to see which area prints best. The plate shouldn't be too sticky, but neither should it be as dry as when printing with ink.

To print in intaglio and relief is a bit tricky with wetter media, but with practice it can be achieved. The areas of intaglio and relief on the plate must be very clearly defined, with enough space so that it is possible to paint liberally into the crevices in order to leave sufficient dye.

This is done as follows:
1. First, push the thickened dye into the nooks and crannies of the plate with a sponge paintbrush.
2. With a large ball of tarlatan or a clean sponge paintbrush, wipe the thickened dye off the relief surface of the plate.
3. Then, with a sponge paintbrush or a roller, paint the relief surface of the plate with the second color.
4. Print as before. When printing fabrics with dyes through the press, remember to put one or two pieces of fabric on top of the fabric to be printed before placing the felts, otherwise the dye will bleed through to them. A piece of paper or craft paper can be placed underneath the felts for extra security.

Changing print media

The method of simultaneous color printing only works when using a single medium. In order to change the print medium from a water-based medium to an oil-based one or vice versa, or from inks to fabric paints or dyes, the plate will need to be cleaned thoroughly first and left to dry. For practical reasons and ease of cleaning, it is better to print with the water-based medium first and then use the oil-based medium to finish off the plate.

Clean the plate between prints as follows:
1. Print off one last print onto craft paper to reduce the amount of ink present.
2. Now clean off the ink, using water if appropriate, or vegetable oil or the necessary solvent if oil-based ink has been used. Try to use as little wet medium as possible when cleaning the plate as it is difficult to be really sure how well the glues and materials applied to it will stand up to the process, especially if cardboard has been used as a base. Vegetable oil works better if left on the oil-based ink for five to fifteen minutes before being cleaned off.
3. To get into the difficult areas, try using a toothbrush.
4. Once clean, leave to dry naturally so that the plate remains as flat as possible.

Different types of press

Although in the instructions I refer to a roller-style etching press for the color techniques described, a screw-down woodblock printing press can also be used, and may possibly produce prints in intaglio and relief if the plate is suitable and if enough pressure can be achieved. The techniques described in this section may therefore be attempted with a screw-down hand press and even with a car! Proceed in exactly the same way as described in the previous chapter (see pages 81–83), working with the color techniques described on page 93. Remember to use felts to provide flexibility in order for the paper to mold around the plate. Pivoting hand presses can also be used, but weights or screw systems will be needed to achieve a good level of pressure. Although the screw-down hand press provides less pressure than an etching press, the results can still be very good. More information is given on this type of press in Chapter 9.

Drying the print

Special care may be needed when drying a print to prevent the paper deforming. This problem occurs if the paper was particularly wet when printed, or if there was a very large amount of pressure used to make the print. Prints can be left to dry naturally in the first place to see how they are going to behave. If they have not dried flat, a good technique is to dampen them with a light spray of water, interleave them with tissue paper, and leave them to dry slowly under a wooden board, such as plywood, with a weight on top. If using water-based ink, do make sure that the ink is absolutely dry before spraying the print with water to flatten it; oil-based ink won't cause any problems.

With experience you will discover which prints are more likely to buckle on drying than others – large prints, for example, have a greater tendency to do so. In this case, when the paper is still wet, tape it on all four sides to a board with brown pre-glued paper tape (the type that needs wetting in order to stick), just as you would to stretch watercolor paper. This is then left to dry. The paper will shrink as it dries and the print will become flat and tight.

Finishing off

The prints will now need to be numbered and signed. A good practice is to put numbers on the very edge of the paper as they come off the press. Once the printing has finished, the number of prints made will be known and they can then be numbered – 1/10, 2/10 and so on if there were ten prints made; 1/15, 2/15 and so on if there were fifteen prints made, for example. If the print run is not finished, estimate and decide on the number of prints that are going to be achieved, so that the prints can be numbered. After the number, write the title of the print if there is one, and then your signature. Use a pencil for the whole process to show that it is done by hand.

Of course, many collagraph prints are so much more like one-offs than a series of prints that it may be legitimate to call an individual print an artist's proof or, in the case of several prints, even serial monoprints, as they are all different. But when prints are inked and pulled individually from the same plate the print is considered a multi-original medium, so collagraphs, however different, printed from the same plate can legitimately be numbered as in any other multi-original printing process.

If you don't wish to number the prints, they could be marked A. P. (artist's proof), although technically, this is used to signify extra prints that were made during the printing for the artist, who has the right to make ten percent more prints than the print run specified. In French the term is E. A. (*épreuve artiste*), which can be seen on some of the prints in this book.

At the beginning of my collagraphy practice I found the notion of numbering prints a little over-fussy – after all, they are not identical, like etchings – but I have since persuaded myself that for collagraphy to be taken seriously in the print and art world the numbering system needs to be adhered to. Someone who acquires a print has the right to know how many were made.

Fossil I. This shows the print, attached with brown paper tape, drying on a board.

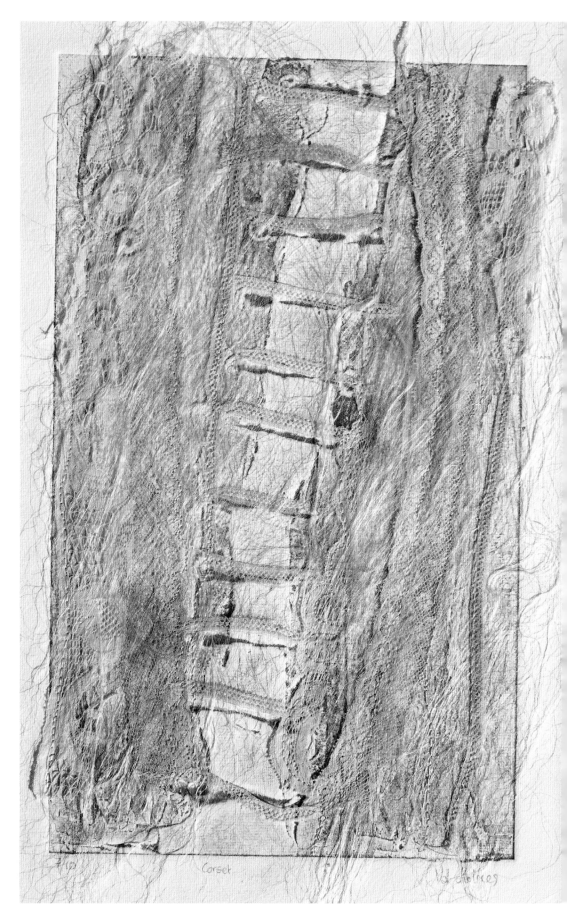

Corset. This shows the numbering, title and signature system for marking printed works. This particular print has had lace and fine silk–fibre paper added with stitching.

CHAPTER 6

EMBROIDERING THE PRINT

Developing the printed image

Not every surface that looks interesting will print well – very often things can look unclear and messy when they turn up in print, as already discussed. Intriguing textures created in print are all very well, but for a print to work there needs to be a fairly clear story – good line and good contrasts. Bear this in mind when creating embroidered and manipulated surfaces on the plate for printing.

With experience you will be able to judge the level of detail on a plate that is necessary to make a good print. In the meantime, any experiments that create interesting texture but are without a clear image or good contrasts need not be consigned to the bin, as further stitching and embroidery can be added to create a more successful result.

As we have seen, a collagraphy plate, unless very well protected with hard varnish, will produce about ten to twenty prints. Even if made with just one color, the prints may vary as the materials glued or stitched to the plate gradually get flattened by the pressure of the press or the rubbing to which they are subjected. For this reason it is difficult to print a classic edition in which all the prints are identical – but this offers the opportunity to experiment instead.

Fossil I. The print on linen fabric was embellished with dyed cotton scrim using an Embellisher machine, and then stitched.

If working with one simple color, it can be interesting to print on a variety of different paper and textile surfaces (see Chapter 2), rather than just one, in which case certain pieces could be used for embroidery experimentation.

If different colors have been used, with the methods described in Chapter 5, some of the developed color prints may be excellent, but some of them may not be developed enough, so could benefit from additional work.

When I look at a collection of prints that I have made from a collagraphy plate, I find that some are good paper works in their own right and really need nothing else added to them, whereas others are disappointing in some way and require more treatment. This provides a new challenge, a chance to be inspired by the print and to continue experimenting with the image. Working in this way I can go in many directions: paper prints can be stitched on, have other materials or textures applied to them, and receive any amount of development to enhance the result.

When I make prints on fabric it is with the full intention of adding stitching or other embellishment to them. Printed textile pieces cry out for more embroidery and detail, as printing with inks can often leave the fibers of the fabric very apparent and so more work is necessary to underline certain images, textures, or colors.

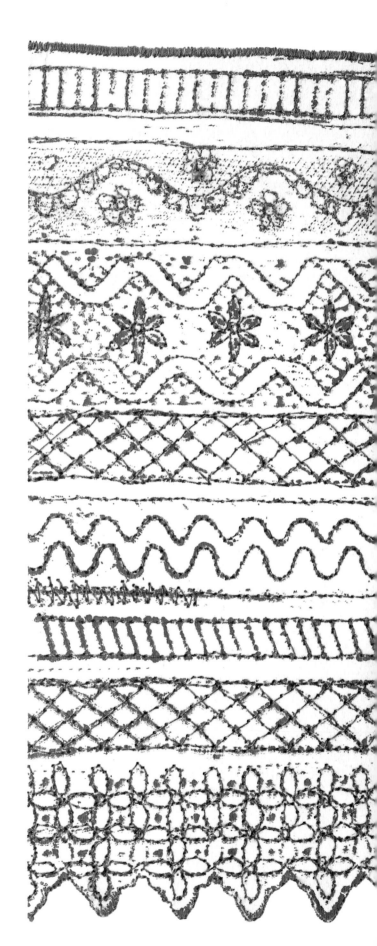

Lace Sampler. Lace samples on a cardboard plate were printed with a spoon on 300gsm etching paper – far too thick to get a good image. The lines of ink were reworked with free-motion machine embroidery.

Fountain. A print from a free-motion embroidered metal plate (see also pages 62 and 63). This was printed on fabric with oil-based ink and then dyes were applied to the fabric. The print could benefit from additional stitching.

The great thing about printing is that it offers a number of similar starting points that can then be explored in order to understand more fully the original marks and textures present in the image. The advantage is evident, as experiments with a single print, and the textile marks and color choices that could be made in relation to it, can result in a series of developed work and a better appreciation of how an image can be treated.

If the original image is realistic in nature, this realism can be enhanced by choosing embroidery to emphasize aspects that will lead to a greater understanding of the image. On the other hand, the original intention of the image could be ignored and the printed marks in it treated simply as abstract elements to inspire something completely new. Conversely, an abstract print may inspire a realism that could be suggested or added to with embroidery. The richness of the textures and marks present in the print may also offer inspiration that could lead to the addition of a small amount of stitching or other materials, or the whole surface could be treated in a new way, leaving very little of the original print visible.

Urban Landscape. A piece of linen sheeting, which had been left in the print studio and used as a cleaning rag for inks, was passed through the press with this plate. The print was embroidered and repaired with handstitching and machine embroidery.

Venice. Image from a plate made with stitched plastic (see also *Venice* on pages 56 and 89). A cotton backing was added to the paper before the stitching was worked with free-motion machine stitching. The black lines of the print were left unstitched as they resemble machine stitching.

Refugees. Image from a cardboard plate with dripped glue (see also *Refugees* on pages 79 and 95), printed on paper. The figures of the refugees were simply outlined with a free-motion stitch.

Embroidery on paper prints

Stitching or textile elements can easily be added to a paper print. If there are concerns about the solidity of the paper in relation to the amount of stitching that is likely to be added, it may be a good idea to back it first. An ordinary cotton fabric will do for this, but Pellon interfacing, thin felt, or a nonwoven fabric could also be considered. For very fine papers, a fine silk fabric would be a better choice so as not to spoil the delicate quality of the paper. Vanishing muslin, a fabric that turns brown, disintegrates, and brushes off after being heated with an iron or heat tool, could also be useful if you want to remove the protective fabric afterwards to preserve a very fine paper – but take care not to scorch the paper when burning off the muslin.

With proper protection any amount of stitching can be added by machine, so experiment with different prints to see how they can be exploited with stitching, embroidery, or even some appliqué. The machine needle will be blunted from stitching into paper, so it is best to change it after using it in this way. A good idea is to keep a labeled needle box especially for needles that have been used on paper or metal.

Handstitching onto paper is less likely to tear it, but be careful about the thickness of the thread used. If this is thick and the stitches are relatively dense, it might be worth supporting the paper with a fabric before stitching. Try to choose one that is easy to stitch into, as the needle may already be difficult enough to get through the paper.

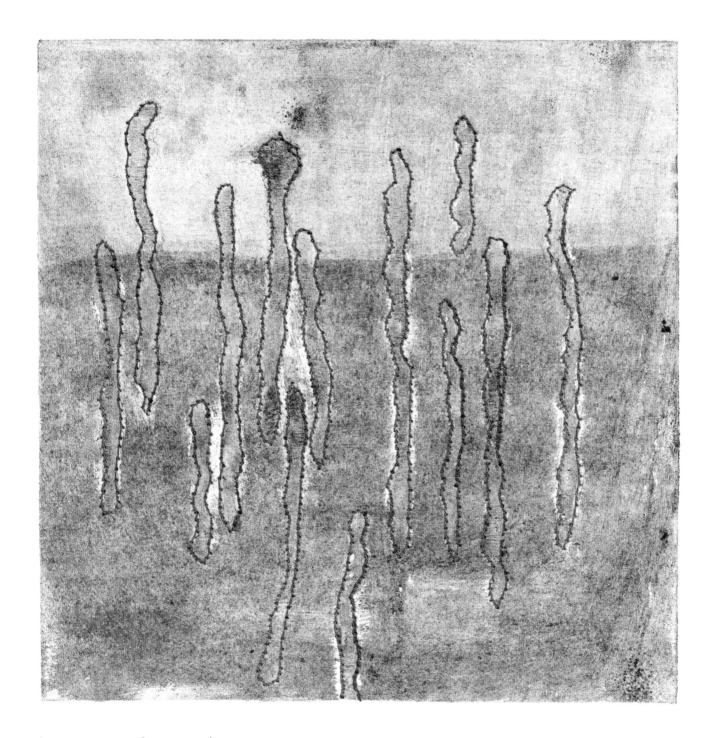

Inspiration for stitching

To help you to build up a general understanding of how prints can be developed and embellished, try the following exercises with different prints off the same plate to see where they could lead:

• Carefully choose a few lines to enhance on the print in order to bring an image or collection of marks into focus.

• Look at the textures created on the plate and think what kind of stitching could be added to enhance them.

• Stitch over most of the image – scribble coloring-in stitches with free-motion machine stitching, or use long individual handstitches to imitate crosshatching.

• Use the print as a starting point only, perhaps allowing the color and textures to influence you. Add bits of fabric and stitching to cover nearly all of the print, or the whole of it.

Stitching on textile prints

Fabric prints do look better if there is more to them than just the inked image. Adjustments can be made before the printing process by altering the fabrics in the ways suggested in Chapter 2. Techniques such as dyeing, patching, or stitching may create a fabric sufficiently interesting once printed to need no further embellishment. However, even on altered fabrics additional work may be appropriate, so look at the print to decide how to add to it in order to clarify the image or, conversely, how to disguise it in a mass of stitching. If the fabric is fine, try backing it with interfacing, so that stitching can be done without an embroidery hoop.

Make a number of prints on fabric from the same plate, using the same or different colors. It will be more interesting, from a working point of view, if the colors vary, so that you will have more ideas to play with. Try the following exercises to understand just how differently a print and image can look according to the choice of embellishment added:

- Carefully choose a few lines to enhance on the print in order to bring an image or collection of marks into focus.
- Look at the textures created on the plate and ask yourself what kind of stitching could be added to enhance them.
- Stitch over most of the image – scribble coloring-in stitches with free-motion machine embroidery, or use long individual hand stitches to imitate crosshatching. Running stitch or seed stitch can be worked into the textures created by printing in a very satisfactory way (see *Venice* on page 104).
- Use the print as a starting point only, perhaps allowing the color and textures to influence you. Add fabric and stitching to embellish the print.

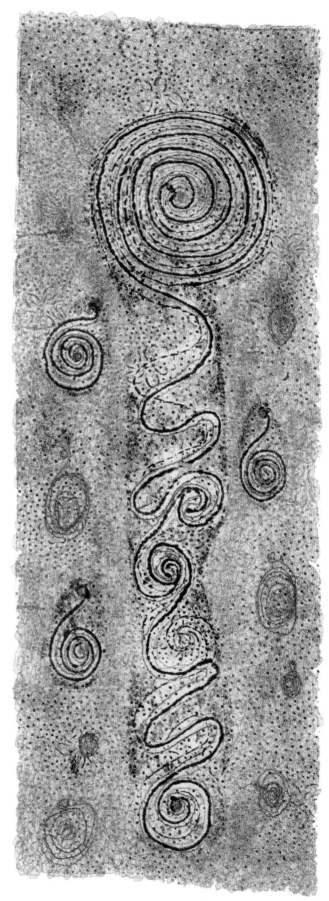

The Sun's Tale. This was printed on linen, then embroidery in gold thread was stitched over the whole background and details picked out in a thicker colored thread.

Wood. This was printed on acrylic felt, which was stitched to a paper version of the same print, following the lines of the design. The felt was then heated with a heat tool.

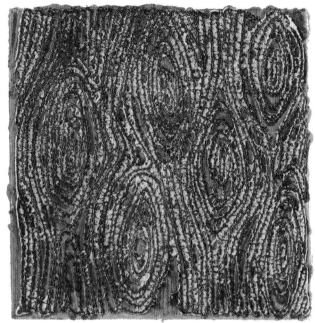

Wood. This shows the print burnt back with a heat tool after stitching.

- Carefully decide how the print could be developed with appliqué, using small or larger bits of fabric. Keep the work reserved and orderly.
- What about the Embellisher machine? Try working from the front to create lines and movement. Try working from the back with fabrics or fibers. The points of color created on the front when working from the back of the print could enhance the textures already present.
- Beads, buttons, ribbons, and so on could all find their way onto a printed image.
- Try metallic transfer foil on iron-on fusible webbing or on the adhesive powder Supermend. This product is like powdered iron-on webbing and when used with metallic transfer foil it takes up just small amounts of foil to add bits of sparkle to the work. To do this, sprinkle some Supermend powder onto the fabric print, place the transfer foil, metallic side up, on top of this, and then add some baking parchment to protect the iron. Use an iron on a medium to hot setting to transfer the foil. Allow this to cool, and then carefully pull off the baking parchment and the foil to leave behind the sparkly bits. The print must be absolutely dry before you do this or more foil may stick to the ink than envisaged. Stitching could then be added.

Printing onto heatable surfaces

Printing onto surfaces that can be heated with a heat tool or cut with a soldering iron can add to your repertoire of interesting effects. Synthetic felt gives good results when printed on, and Tyvek fabric also responds to printing. Once printed, try heating these fabrics to see what textures will be produced, or stitch them first to create a resist to the heating process. Particularly interesting effects can be achieved with synthetic felt, where small, close stitching creates interesting textures and holes when heated sufficiently afterwards with a heat tool. These textures could be an appropriate way of pushing the print's initial textural qualities even further.

Textile and embroidery techniques are so wide and varied. Each individual artist has his or her own repertoire of favourite stitches and techniques; try out yours on your prints so that they reflect your personal style and way of working.

CHAPTER ‹ 7 ›
COLLAGRAPHY FOR PAPER RELIEF

Printing blind

Collagraph plates can produce wonderful effects simply by being printed blind – that is, without any ink at all. To exploit this technique it is best to use the plate before ink has been put on it for any other printing. There are two reasons for this: first, once a slow-drying ink has been on the plate, unless the plate has been cleaned meticulously, it will be necessary to wait a few days to be sure that there will be no trace of ink on the blind print; and second, the plate will be at its most detailed and in its best relief form for blind printing before it undergoes too much pressure from inking and printing. To get the best effects, make sure that the plate has good relief and texture, and use paper with long fibers.

Working with an etching press

Very good results can be obtained very simply. Start by wetting and then partially drying the paper as usual, so that it is evenly damp. Place the plate face up on the bed of the press, put the paper on top and the felts on top of that, and then roll the whole piece through the press. The felts will allow the paper to be pressed well into the plate to form the relief. In a screw-down hand press the results will also be good – use felts in a similar way.

Some plates print well if inked in some areas and left blind in others, so the textures can speak for themselves.

San Gimignano. The heavily textured areas were printed blind. The colored areas were inked separately, using a dry brush and oil–based ink.

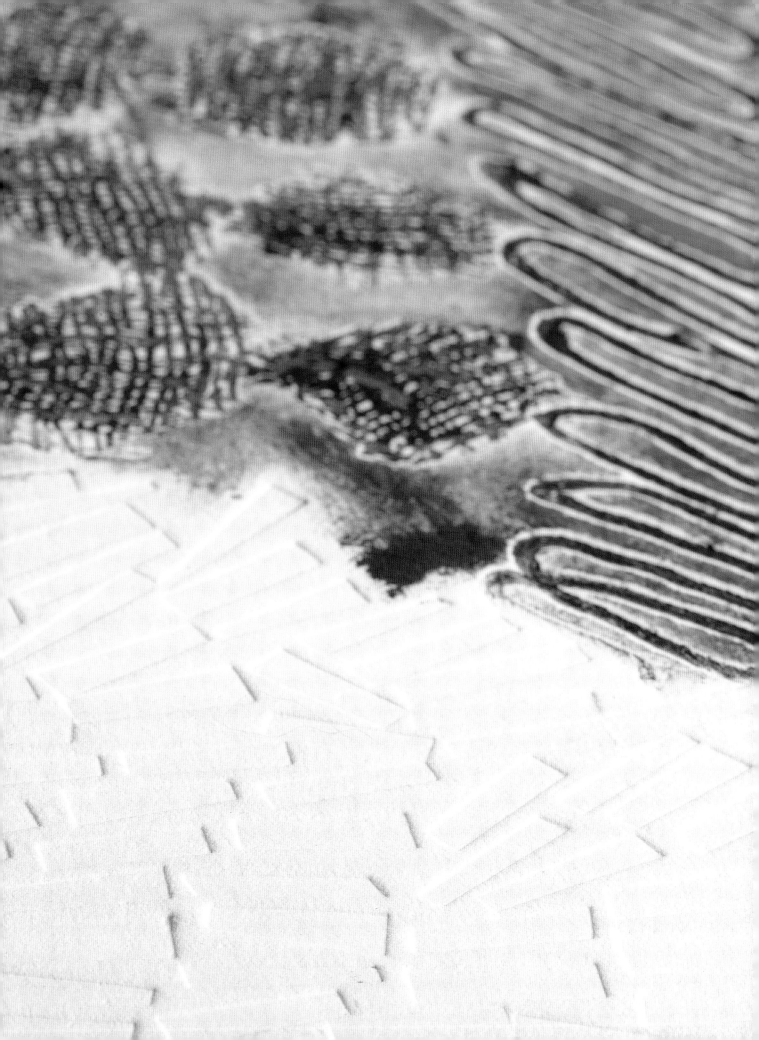

Smocking. This was worked from a metal plate on a screw-down hand press. See also *Smocking* on pages 69 and 83.

Working with handmade paper

To obtain even more detail and relief, especially if a press is not available, it can be a good idea to use freshly made handmade paper. If you are familiar with the process of making your own paper and have the equipment, that's great; if not, below is an easy version, using basic paper-making equipment, to get you started.

You will need:
- A mold and deckle – this special frame for making sheets of paper can be bought from a number of suppliers. Alternatively, if you just want to try this out, use a splash guard for frying pans – the sheet of paper will be round, though!
- A deep tray – a cat-litter tray may be big enough. The frame should fit into it, but if it doesn't, don't worry as we can get over that one too!
- A blender, although with patience you can manage without this.
- Waste paper. For moulding it is better if the paper has long fibers, so either buy cotton-rag paper specially made for paper-making or collect all the offcuts of your prints on watercolor and etching paper. These can be mixed with a little ordinary waste paper, but try to keep the long-fibre paper content high.
- Felt.

Method:
1. Prepare the plate beforehand by carefully covering it with clingfilm to prevent the paper sticking to its surface once the paper has been made.
2. Soak the waste paper, torn into small pieces, in lots of water for at least two hours or overnight.

Working without a press

This is a little more difficult and the best way forward is to try to organize a suitable alternative – the car, the garden roller or a flower press with felts in order to obtain the same degree of relief possible with a press. If it isn't possible to use any of these items, proceed as follows:

1. Soak the paper for fifteen minutes; use a long-fiber etching paper if possible.
2. Cover the plate as neatly as you can with clingfilm. This is necessary as the paper can sometimes stick to the plate.
3. Place the plate face up, then put the wet paper and two or three felts on top under something very heavy. This could be a board, a piece of plywood, or chipboard to spread the load evenly followed with weights on top, or alternatively, you could use an item of furniture.
4. Leave this in place until dry.
5. Remove the weights and felts, and take the paper off the plate. If it is not completely dry, leave it to dry naturally.

3. Mix the soaked paper in the blender. Make sure that you use lots of water with not too much paper so as not to damage the blender. Purchased cotton-rag paper for paper-making can fall apart quite easily if soaked overnight, so this is ideal if you haven't got a blender. Just rub it between your hands to try to break it down into fibers as much as possible.

4. Put this mixture in the tray and submerge the mold and deckle or splash guard in it. Allow the paper pulp to re-form over the mold, then carefully pull out the mold. If you do not have a big enough tray, put the pulp into a jug and pour it over the mold, trying to create as even a surface as possible. If using a deckle, take it off at this stage.

5. Take a piece of felt, place it on top of the freshly made paper, push down to squeeze out as much water as possible, and then flip the paper over. If you are a novice, you will find this much easier than trying to couch – that is, lay down your paper onto a table of felts.

6. Take the felt with the paper on it and place it paper side down on top of the collagraphic plate. Ease the paper into the textures and molding of the plate, if possible with the felt still in place.

7. Take off the felt if you can and allow the paper to dry. If the felt is too attached, it can be left in place to dry, but this will take longer.

Other materials can be included in the paper for more interesting effects. Threads or bits of fiber or fabric, plant materials such as leaves, dried flowers, or small pieces of newspaper can either be added to the pulp itself or accurately placed onto the mold (face down) before the paper pulp is added. When the paper is removed from the mold the included objects will be embedded into it on the textured side of the paper.

Rope. A blind print of heavy cords on a cardboard plate.

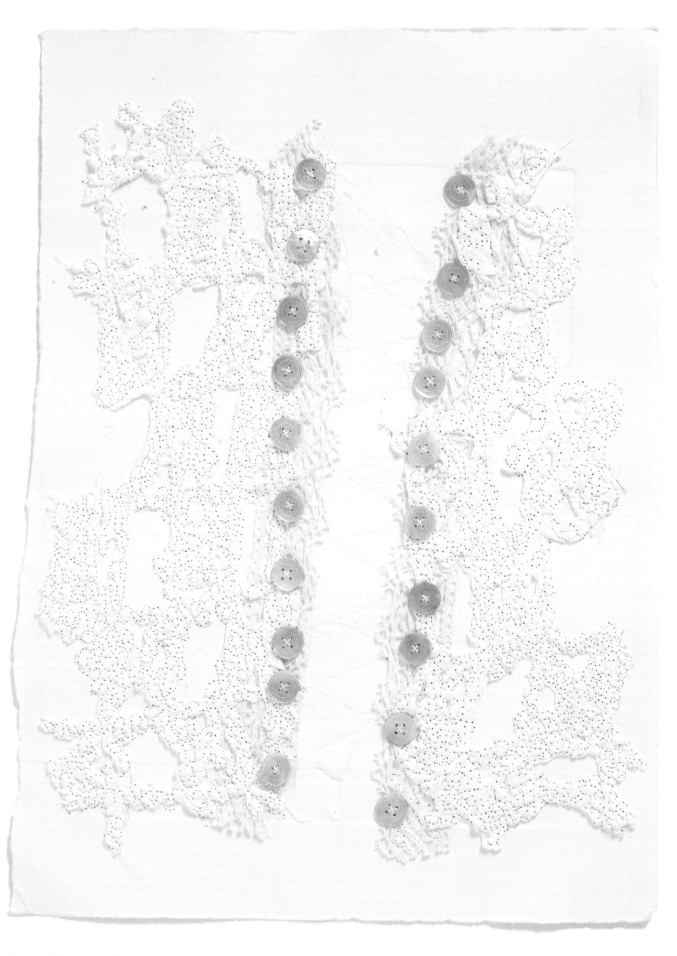

Including paper relief in embroidered surfaces

The paper used for the following techniques could be colored first. Dyes, watercolors or inks could be used for sheets of paper. For the hand-made paper method ink or dyes could be added to the pulp mix, or colored paper could be included. However, the relief will be better appreciated if the paper is left white, as the contours and textures will be more clearly seen.

If your plans would benefit from color, though, try rubbing pastels (soft or oil) or gold bronzing powders into the surface of the paper to highlight certain areas of texture. This will be more successful if the paper already has a base color on it.

The resulting piece, whether white or colored, might be acceptable as it is and may not need further work; but if the intention is to include it in other embroidery work, some precautions may need to be taken:

• If the paper has been pressed into the collagraphy plate, consider backing it with a fabric before stitching into the desired surface – unless this surface is a textile itself and will offer the required support.

• For handmade paper, which may be a little fragile, brush over it with a generous pasting of cornstarch glue (see the recipe on page 49), or use acrylic wax to protect it before stitching.

Quilting effects

The quilted appearance of the paper could be echoed by using quilting effects produced by stitching. Make sure that any embroidery enhances the textures and relief – work into the flatter areas or between the textures.

Integrating the paper relief print

The paper relief print could either be incorporated into a textile surface, or textiles and embroidery could be applied to the paper relief. Simple appliqué techniques might be effective where the notion of one element applied to another may give a deliberate sense and meaning to the work. Patching and patchwork can have strong cultural references. If these techniques aren't appropriate, try using stitching and color to integrate the different surfaces fully so that they work together.

Corset. A blind print was made from the same plate as *Fossil I* (see page 101). Lace made with paper pulp was applied with free-motion embroidery and mother-of-pearl buttons were added.

Smocking. Hand embroidery was added to pre-punched metal, and a blind print was worked on a screw-down hand press. See page 110.

CHAPTER ‹ 8 ›

THE MONOPRINT AND COLLAGRAPHY

The monoprint

The defining feature of a monoprint is that there is just one example printed off a surface that has been marked or painted with an artist's medium before printing.

The technique was developed using oil paint applied to a glass ground, but any non-absorbent ground will do. It is important that a slow-drying medium is used. The paint is worked onto the surface to create the desired image, and the paper is placed on top. The work is then either passed through a press (although not if glass has been used) or pressed using a roller. For more textural interest the paper can be placed onto the painted surface and pressed down unevenly, using mark-making instruments such as a pencil or palette knife. The marks made on the paper produce different tonalities, rather than the whole image as drawn on the plate. The technique can also be used on fabric, using fabric paints or thickened dyes.

Artists often produce a second image from the same source, either by using more or different pressure, or by using a solvent that liquefies the paint in order to produce a paler image.

Sunflower Field. This monoprint was painted on glass with thickened dye and an imprint made on the fabric with a roller. The blunt edge of a paintbrush was then used to draw pressure marks on the fabric to enable it to receive more dye (see image on page 116).

This technique has a huge advantage in that a press is really not required to obtain good results, and you can experiment with a roller or mark-making tools to great effect. It can be used to make unique prints on paper or fabric and also as a starting point for an embroidery or textile work. Of course, the monoprint is also a work that can stand alone and not require further development.

Using a paintbrush to make pressure marks on the fabric, when making *Sunflower Field* (shown on page 115).

Using textured surfaces

Although glass is traditionally used for this technique, textured surfaces can also provide interesting results. Sand or carborundum paper, or any other textured surfaces that are not too absorbent, can be a starting point for the painting. The painted surface and the paper or fabric can be put through a press or rubbed off either by using a roller or baren, or by the drawing technique.

An adaptation of this technique can be used with collagraphy plates. The plate provides a textural surface that can be painted on with an appropriate medium. The painting may cover the whole plate or only parts of it. This can then be passed through the press, or printed with a roller or whatever other means seem suitable. The plate can then be re-inked in a different way and another print taken. The term "serial monoprint" seems appropriate for this method of working, particularly because, on the images shown on pages 118 and 119, the inking had little to do with the actual imagery on the plate. Using large quantities of thickened dye, as in the first print (page 119), meant that there was little reference to the original textures of the plate.

This shows a painting, made with thickened dye, on the glass and the imprint made on the fabric.

After pressure with a roller the image is more marked on the fabric.

Port. A serial monoprint from carborundum paper. Oil-based ink was applied to the large-format carborundum paper with a roller. A print was then taken before more ink was added and another print made. This print is the third in the series.

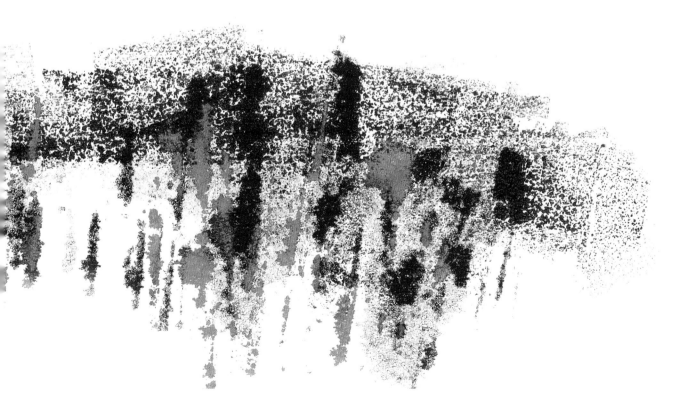

Port. Dye remained on the plate after the first print (opposite), so another piece of fabric was placed on top and this time put under an etching press to pick up the last quantities of dye from the plate. The stitching on top is very light.

Port. The fabric was printed once again from the collagraph plate with dye on it and then stitched by hand.

Lights in the Port. Thickened dye was generously applied to a collagraph plate, the fabric was added, and the image was transfered with a roller. The result was worked on with an Embellisher machine and stitched.

Media for the monoprint

The media that can be used for this technique are the same as for collagraph printing. It is best to use a medium that will stay wet long enough for the plate to be made, and for any mark-making that transfers the color to the paper or fabric to occur.

Using thickened dye on fabric can produce interesting results. Experiment with the quantities of dye that you use – the color may or may not bleed and this may or may not be interesting. Try different quantities of thickened dye and different methods of printing.

Leftover ink rolled out onto the glass plate for printing may also provide an interesting starting point for a monoprint, and would also prevent wasted ink. Paper can be applied and a drawing made through it to create a monoprint.

CHAPTER ‹ 9 ›
THE PRESS

Practical alternatives

As we have seen, collagraph prints can be made without a press, but the results with a press are interesting and wonderful – and easier. Unfortunately, a press can be an expensive investment and will also require permanent installation, so some studio space is essential. Before taking such a step, however, there are some other solutions you can try that will enable you to work on a press just when you need to. After all, the creation of a plate, and the work that you may do on the resulting prints, will be more time-consuming than the actual printing. With good advance preparation, a session on a press from time to time could be satisfactory.

One solution is to contact a local art school to see if they have etching classes and a press that you could use in class conditions. Another solution might be to find a local etcher who is willing to share his or her press, or hire it out from time to time. In this situation it would be a good idea to have your own felts, inks, tarlatan and so on, and to take along your own pre-dampened paper in a large plastic bag, so as to impose as little as possible on someone else's studio space, and to be able to work most efficiently.

It is worth looking at the second-hand marketplace too, and even at certain new presses. Some lightweight presses are not that expensive, and although these may be barely adequate for good etchings, they may well be fine for printing collagraphs because they require less pressure.

Instructions can be found online for building all kinds of presses. There are detailed plans on my website (see page 127), but there are many others.

City Street with Three Trees Old cloth was used with added pieces of corded pin tucking. The trees were worked on Thermogauze (vanishing muslin) with satin stitch and glued on.

A flower press

A flower press is particularly easy to make and does not require much equipment or a great deal of skill. The results of relief printing on a flower press are good, although of course it really doesn't provide enough pressure for intaglio printing. It can, however, also be used to press the collagraphs once made – simply layer them between pieces of tissue paper, screw down the press and let them dry slowly. This way they will dry flat. If there is a lot of relief in the printed paper though, it is best to let the prints dry naturally without pressure.

A flower press can also be used to press handmade paper – and even flowers!

You will need:
• 2 pieces of scrap plywood or chipboard – not too large or they won't create enough pressure. Pieces measuring 14" × 11" (35 × 27 cm) will allow you to print on letter-size paper
• Drill with bit to match screw size
• Four 4" (10 cm) flat-head screws
• 8 washers
• Felt, synthetic felt, or old blankets cut to the same size as the pieces of wood, with the corners cut at an angle to avoid the screws
• 4 wing nuts
• Varnish (optional)

Method:
1. Cut both pieces of wood to the desired size.
2. Drill a hole in each corner of the wood pieces, using a bit the same size as the screws.
3. Put the four screws through the holes in one of the pieces of wood, with four of the washers underneath. This will be the bottom of the press.
4. Reserve the other piece of wood, the pieces of felt, the wing nuts and the other four washers – these will all be placed on top of the protruding screws when the materials to be pressed are in place.
5. If you find this type of press satisfactory for the kind of work you do, you may consider varnishing the wood to help it to cope with any dampness transmitted by the paper, dyes or inks.

A screw-down hand press

This is the second easiest type of press to make. For a press of this kind you will need to be able to cut and weld metal, as the nuts on the press ideally require welding. This press can be used to dry prints, flatten hand-made paper or dry flowers, as above. It will give good results for relief printing and, depending on the plate, may also be used for some intaglio printing.

The way in which this press works is simple. A flat, unmovable wooden baseplate is constructed within a metal frame. Above this baseplate another piece of wood of the same dimensions is suspended within the frame, supported by the screw. The screw action of the press allows for this suspended wooden plate to descend towards the baseplate in order to exert the necessary pressure, or to be raised in order to insert or remove the collagraph plate and the print. Detailed plans can be found on many online sites, including my own (see page 127).

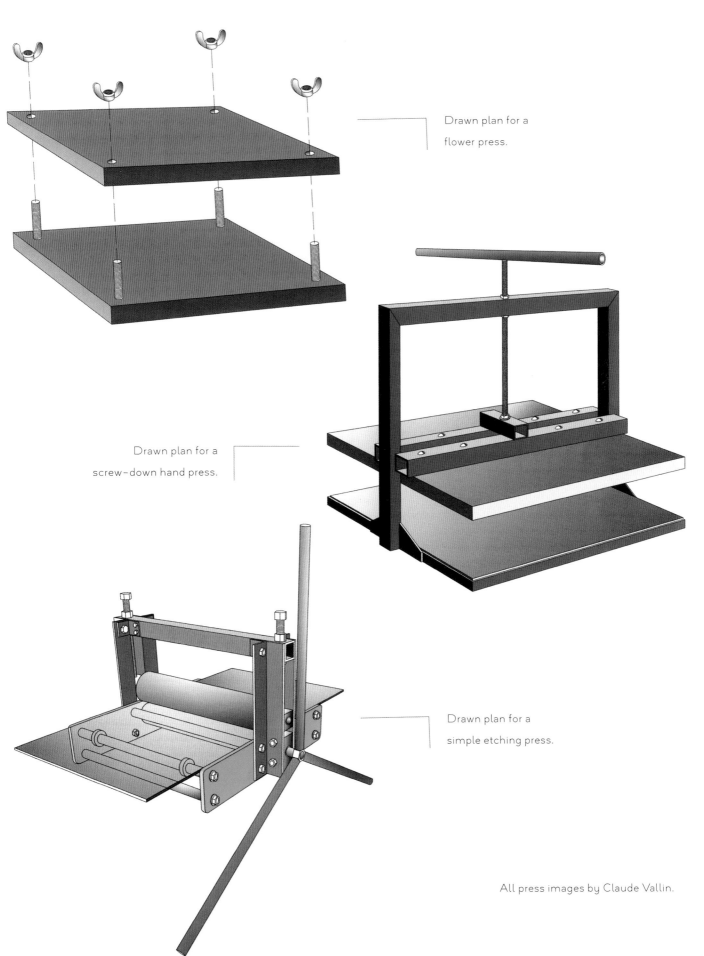

Drawn plan for a
flower press.

Drawn plan for a
screw-down hand press.

Drawn plan for a
simple etching press.

All press images by Claude Vallin.

An etching press

The ideal type of press is an etching press, and with a small amount of engineering skill it is possible to build one for a very reasonable cost. The outline plan on page 123 is for the first press that Claude, my etching husband, built for use with copper and zinc etchings. With the help of various friends and a cousin with a metal lathe, the total cost of the press was counted in bottles of wine for everyone, rather than actual cash! Detailed plans are available on my website (see page 127), but you will find many other websites and videos that fully explore the construction of such a press. So, look at your own skills and those of the people you know – perhaps it's possible; it's not as complicated as all that. A metal lathe is necessary to make the rollers, a welder to weld the bolts and the tubes for the arms of the press, and a drill to make the holes. You will also need the correct equipment to cut the metal parts to size.

The way in which an etching press works is very simple: a flat bed of metal moves between two metal rollers under pressure. One of these rollers is turned by a wheel, or metal bars, and it is this that causes the flat bed to move along between the rollers. The plate to be printed, with the paper on top and the felts on top of that, is placed on the flat bed and this passes through the rollers under pressure to create the print. The most important parts of a press are the two rollers, which must be perfectly cylindrical.

Prints with collagraph plates don't always need a great deal of pressure and quite often – or at least for the first few prints off a plate – the weight of the roller may be sufficient. Bolts added to the frame of the press will increase the pressure produced by the top roller, if necessary. However, with more pressure it becomes more difficult to turn the press, so the arms of the wheel that does this can be lengthened to diminish the effort required. Alternatively, a gearing system with gears or chains can be engaged to help to turn the press, but this is more complicated. A press with a direct action can work quite satisfactorily if the size of the press is not too big.

Many professional etching presses even have motors attached to them so that they don't have to be turned by hand. Such presses have warning systems to prevent fingers getting crushed between the rollers! This type of press may be fine for traditionally etched plates that are all the same depth and therefore always go through the press in exactly the same way from start to finish; but with collagraph plates the amount of pressure required on a plate can change quite rapidly between the first print and the tenth, as the plate is gradually flattened. Moreover, one plate may require a certain kind of treatment but the following one may need more or less pressure because of the objects used, or because of its depth. For these reasons a hand-turned press seems a better option for collagraph prints, as the pressure exerted on the plate can be felt with every turn of the press.

Once the workings of the press have been understood, the plans shown here could be modified with respect to the dimensions and technology of the press.

Never forget that these machines are heavy and should be used with prudence. Working alone, without distractions, will help to ensure that fingers don't get trapped between the rollers. Do adopt safe working conditions so that the press won't fall and won't crush fingers – consider fixing it to a solid, robust table for safety and ease of use. Keep the press clean between printing sessions and cover it with a dust cloth when not in use.

Printing is fascinating, whatever method is used – it is always exciting to lift up the paper and see the resulting print from a plate. With collagraphy there are even more unknowns, and the opportunity to play with colours keeps this sense of excitement alive for every single print.

CONCLUSION

Discovering collagraphy

Having Claude, a traditional etcher, as a husband was how I first got involved in printing. He built our presses, introduced me to the medium and encouraged my appreciation of etching. A local etcher, who had experimented with etching on tin cans with almost stitch-like marks, was the next influence in creating my desire to produce prints that had a resonance with my textile-art practice as well as my drawings. After the first few experiments I was hooked, and I have continued experimenting ever since, including both traditional and 20th-century etching techniques of color application with my own techniques of producing plates for printing.

When I started out I felt very much on my own with my experimentation, but that's how I advance and how I like working. I learnt how to accept the plates that didn't give me the results I was looking for as part of the learning process, sometimes accepting the result as satisfactory despite this, and sometimes realizing that a particular way of using a certain material was just inappropriate for the medium of printing.

Exploiting prints in your work

I have shown that good results can be produced without an etching press, and you may be quite happy with the results you can achieve in this way. But it is also true that if you enter fully into printing and producing multiple prints, at some time a press will become a highly desirable object, so I wish you luck in your search for one or in constructing your own press.

In this book there is a lot of advice that will hopefully prove useful and will allow you to produce interesting prints more easily. If you are first and foremost a textile artist, the information about how prints can inspire the inclusion of stitching and textile techniques should help to make collagraphy relevant to your work.

Collagraphy as an art form is still in its early days, however, and there is so much more to find out, so the information here should be used as just a springboard for your own trail of discovery. There are, as I have said before, as many ways of responding to collagraphy as there are practitioners, so I hope that you will also find a way of personalizing this technique to make it an integral part of your own work.

GLOSSARY

Acrylic ink Ink of a creamy consistency, used for lino printing.

Acrylic paste There is a huge variety of acrylic pastes on the market. When mixed with various additives, these enable you to create all sorts of surfaces, from smooth to very rough, all of which can be useful for making collagraphic plates.

Acrylic gel medium A very smooth acrylic paste that cleans off particularly well when making rubs or wiping back ink colours.

Acrylic varnish This acrylic-based varnish for protecting paintings can also protect collagraph plates.

Aqua forte An etching technique for metal plates. The metal is varnished, the varnish is drawn into and the plate is then put into an acid bath to dissolve the metal where the varnish has been removed. The phrase in Italian means "strong water," referring to the acid bath. The plate is inked to the different depths of the indentations that have been created, and, when used with an etching press, the technique will make an intaglio print.

Baren A tool used for hand printing, mainly in relief.

Brodagraphy Invented name for collagraphy using embroidery in the construction of the plate.

Burnishing Action of rubbing with a baren, spoon or other tool to create a print by hand from a plate.

Carborundum powder Fine resistant mineral powder used in collagraphy and etching.

Collagraphy Printing from a plate that has been made by adding things to the plate, rather than removing them as in other printing methods.

Direct engraving Using a tool, rather than acid, to create lines and marks on a metal plate.

Dolly A piece of fabric, usually tarlatan, with a ball of fabric on the inside, which forms a structure a little like a rag doll's head. It is used to add ink to a plate or to rub the ink back off a plate to create nuances of colour.

Embellisher machine A machine, resembling a sewing machine, that is used for felting fibres together.

Emery paper Paper made with carborundum powder (see above).

Etching Using acid or a specialized tool to mark a metal plate with a design that can be used for intaglio printing on an etching press.

Fabric medium Acrylic-based medium to which pigments or acrylic paint can be added to make fabric paint.

Flower press Simple press usually used for pressing flowers, but which can be used for printing in relief.

Free-motion embroidery Using a normal sewing machine with the feed dog lowered or covered and no foot, or a darning, quilting, or free-motion embroidery foot.

Gesso Thick paint size, usually acrylic-based with a plaster additive. Used to size artists' canvases, but can be used on any surface to protect the base and enable the media used on top to stay on the surface of the base instead of sinking into it.

Glycerine alcohol Used as an additive to acrylic paint to lengthen drying time, glycerine alcohol can be found in cookshops.

Intaglio Method of printing in which the depths of the plate are inked and printed (not the relief).

Marine varnish Waterproof varnish useful for protecting wood surfaces. Can be used to protect the wood on a flower press or for wood-based collagraph plates.

Monoprint Method of printing from a prepared surface where one drawing or painting on the surface produces one print.

Paper The European measurement for describing paper weight measures a single piece of paper with a two-dimensional height and a width of one square metre. This measurement is noted as gsm (or g/m^2, gm/m^2, g/m^2). The measurement may be measuring a hypothetical square metre, but is a good like-for-like measurement because it compares the weights of same-sized papers. The U.S. method of paper weight may be more familiar, but it has its drawbacks when making comparisons. This method gives the weight of the paper as if weighing 500 sheets (or a ream). Differences in the dimensions of paper are not taken into account. Therefore, the U.S. weight of a letter-size paper that is thick and dense may be the same as a poster-size paper that is light and tissue-thin, because 500 sheets of each weigh the same. As this is inappropriate for the papers cited in this book, I have used the European measurements.

Plaster of Paris Basic plaster material available in powder form, which dries very quickly.

Relief printing A plate can be prepared with dips and highs in a number of ways; very often by cutting into a material such as wood, lino or metal, or by adding on other materials in the case of collagraphy. Relief printing is when the highs only are printed.

Rubs A term used for the gradual wiping off of ink from the surface of the plate so that the print will have nuances of the same colour. Different colors can also be added and rubbed or wiped off the plate so that multiple colors and nuances occur.

Shellac or button varnish A particularly strong varnish that can be used to give long-lasting protection to a collagraph plate.

Tarlatan Highly sized cotton muslin.

Thermogauze Cotton muslin treated by a chemical process so that it goes brown and rubs away when heated with a heat tool, oven or iron. Useful as a support when stitching on fine papers. Also called vanishing muslin.

Water-washable ink These inks are relatively new on the market. They are oil-based and behave like oil-based inks, requiring a special oil-based additive for diluting. However, they are treated in such a way that they are washable in water and do not require the usual cleaning agents. This makes them particularly agreeable to use. They have the same drying time as oil-based inks.

SUPPLIERS

U.K.

Kemtex Educational Supplies
Chorley Business & Technology Centre
Euxton Lane
Chorley, Lancashire PR7 6TE
Tel: 01257 230220
www.kemtex.co.uk
Dyes and related chemicals

Art Van Go
1 Stevenage Road
Knebworth
Hertfordshire SG3 6AN
www.artvango.co.uk
General art supplies

Great Art
www.greatart.co.uk
Paper, all inks and etching suppliers

U.S.A.

www.lawrence.co.uk
Etching suppliers, felts, inks, presses.

www.graphicchemical.com
Etching suppliers, felts, inks, presses

www.interweavestore.com
Textile and craft supplies, books, and magazines.

AUSTRALIA

The Thread Studio
www.thethreadstudio.com
Textile suppliers

Neil's Art Store
44–46 Greeves St
Fitzroy, Victoria 3065
Australia
www.e-artstore.net
Art and print suppliers

FRANCE

Val Holmes
textile-art-centre.com.fr
Author's website

INDEX

ACKNOWLEDGEMENTS

Thank you to everyone at Batsford/Anova who believed in this project: I've enjoyed doing every book I've ever written, but this one was a very real pleasure. A very special thank you to Claude, my husband, a traditional etcher, who has encouraged all my trials and inventions even when he thought they wouldn't work! Thank you also to my children Lucy and Joanne, who took some of the pictures. Thank you to Michael Wicks for the majority of the photos: the others are by myself. All work is by the author except the lino prints in the introduction by Claire Fauchard and the etching by Claude Vallin. I also thank Claude for the plans in the final chapter.